# How to successfully
# learn a new language
# in 1 year

By Jason Eyermann

**How to successfully learn a new language in 1 year**
By Jason Eyermann

Layout and book design by Jason Eyermann
Published by Aspire Create Publishing
www.aspirecreatepublishing.co.uk
www.learnalanguagein1year.com
First published May 2015
©2015 Jason Eyermann. All Rights Reserved.

Printed by CreateSpace, An Amazon.com Company



ISBN 978-0-9933022-0-6

# Contents

How to successfully learn a new language in 1 year

*How to successfully*
# learn a new language
## in **1** year

# About this book

This book was written to help a new language learner successfully reach a high conversational level in their chosen language in 12 months.

**Part 1** of this book covers general advice and knowledge about language learning along with information and facts about languages in general.

**Part 2** of this book contains a step by step 4 part guide, which describes the changes that you must make as you progress in learning your new language in order to make your language learning experience a success.

I have used my knowledge and experience gathered

from 15 years worth of language learning to help me write this book. I have also researched deeper into many of the topics discussed in this book for the purposes of writing this book.

# Disclaimer

Learning a new language would not be possible if it were not for all the wonderful language learning resources available on both the internet and in bookshops. Throughout this book I give my recommendations of the many resources that I have used while learning languages that I feel have helped me most to progress in the languages that I was learning at that time in the most effective, efficient and enjoyable way. I am in no way affiliated with any of the products mentioned in this book. In cases where the product was a commercial product, I would have paid for using that product

I list many different websites in this book that I have found useful while learning languages. At the time of writing this book, each of these websites were active; however, it is possible that when you come to read this book, some of these websites may have been taken off-line or they may have a different website address. In cases where I have been made aware of any website address changes, then I will add the new address to this book's accompanying website at www.learnalanguagein1year.com/book-links.php.

# PART ONE

# Who is this book for?

This book is for anyone who wants to learn a new language in an effective, efficient, inexpensive and enjoyable way. Some people spend many years trying to learn a language by using similar methods to what I had used when I first started learning French, 15 years ago. My methods, at that time, were based on how I was taught languages by the teachers at my secondary school. Now that I have improved my methods for learning a language, I now know that for anyone who is trying to learn a language using the same methods that we were using while at school, then the language learner will have less chance of ever reaching a conversational level in that language. I have even spoken with people who have obtained A levels in a language, but they don't seem to have the ability to speak that language in any sort of useful way. I believe they could have learned their desired language quicker and with less expense by simply following the guidance set out in this book.

The methods described in this book require you to study only a little everyday; therefore, if you work full time or you are a full time student in a subject unrelated to languages, then this book is still suited for you.

## Things you need for this 1 year challenge

You will need the motivation, time and willingness to learn a new language. If you *want* to learn a language rather than only learning a language because you are being told to learn a language then you stand a better chance of reaching a higher level. *"a language has to be learnt, it cannot be taught"* is a sentence I have heard in the language learning community many times and I completely agree with this statement. If you put in the time and effort then you will see and feel the results.

While learning anything new, most people will have the motivation and enthusiasm to continue learning for the first few weeks, but this motivation can go up and down as you progress. In later chapters, I talk about methods for getting over periods of low motivation while learning languages.

I wish I could say that learning a language was a free experience, but unfortunately not all of the best resources are free. I will be recommending many books, applications and websites throughout this book that I have tried myself. From these recommendations, I hope you will save money from my advice by avoiding purchasing any resources that have not been helpful to me in the past. I try to give you free options when possible.

You will need your own computer and a good internet connection as many of the resources listed in this book are internet based and in the later stages you will need to use the internet to practice speaking your new language with language partners; therefore, you will also need your own private space, void of any loud noises. A good quality microphone and a pair of good quality headphones is also useful to have as being able to hear words clearly is important. I have purchased personal computers in the past with built in microphones and then I later realised the outputted sound of these microphones were poor quality. Because of this, some of my language partners could not sometimes understand me clearly. You should record a sample of your voice and listen to the playback to test the sound quality of your microphone.

You will also need some A4 notepads for practicing your writing and for making notes. I suggest getting a few good quality notepads that are not going to fall apart after only a few weeks of use. You can use these to write your vocabulary lists.

In order to listen to audio while you are not at your computer you will need access to an MP3 player.

# Why I wrote this book

If someone decides to learn a new language without any research into the process then they may try to learn a language while making the same mistakes that I first made when I started to learn my first foreign language, which was French. Ideas about how to study a language first came to me from the methods that were taught to me during my time at school and I have now come to realise that these methods were not effective. I have written a book that I wish I could have been able to read when I first started to learn French, 15 years ago. Owning a book like this would have saved me many years of unsuccessfully trying to learn

French. I hope that the reader of this book will not only benefit from this book by learning a language quicker, but also enable the reader to enjoy the experience of learning a language and give the reader some insight into what can be gained from learning a second language.

# "I speak English. Why learn a new language?"

Being a native speaker of English is a wonderful thing as there are many millions of non-English speaking people around the world trying to achieve something you had learned effortlessly at a very young age. Most estimates say that approximately 1 billion people are learning English around the globe. English has become arguably the most useful language in the world on many different levels from being able to read almost any book in the world, to dealing in international business, science, trade and finance. So, why would you want to spend some of your time everyday for a year learning another language. I will give reasons in this chapter why being able to speak in another language other than only speaking English will be useful and rewarding.

## Communicate with more people

Government statistics show the number of people who speak English as a native language ranks third overall in the world. Once you include people who have learned English as a second language to a fluent level then English jumps to second place behind Chinese Mandarin. Estimates from the two lists below show the top 15 most widely spoken languages in the world. The first list shows the number of native speakers, while the second list shows the number of native speakers plus people who have learned that language as a second language to a fluent level.

### Total number native speakers
1.    Chinese Mandarin (930 Million)
2.    Spanish (387 Million)
3.    English (365 Million)
4.    Hindi (295 Million)
5.    Standard Arabic (280 Million)
6.    Portuguese (204 Million)
7.    Bengali (202 Million)
8.    Russian (160 Million)
9.    Japanese (127 Million)

10.  Punjabi (96 Million)
11.  German (92 Million)
12.  Javanese (82 Million)
13.  Wu (80 Million)
14.  Indonesian (77 Million)
15.  Telugu (76 Million)
(*Depending on the source these figures vary*)

## Total number of fluent speakers

1.  Chinese Mandarin (1030 Million)
2.  English (760 Million)
3.  Spanish (528 Million)
4.  Hindi (380 Million)
5.  Standard Arabic (354 Million)
6.  Russian (272 Million)
7.  Bengali (250 Million)
8.  Portuguese (217 Million)
9.  Indonesian (163 Million)
10.  Swahili (141 Million)
11.  Japanese (135 Million)
12.  French (119 Million)
13.  German (112 Million)
14.  Filipino (105 Million)
15.  Urdu (104 Million)
(*Depending on the source these figures vary*)

As you can see from the above list, learning one of these languages will greatly increase the number of people you will be able to speak with in the world.

The country and city you live in can also influence your language choice as many cities will have minority communities from particular countries in the world. If you find yourself in this position, then you will have an advantage to learn that language as you should have more opportunities to speak and practice your language with people in your local area and you will also make better connections with your local community by speaking their language.

## Work place advantages

Once you have reached a high enough level in another language to communicate with others using everyday types of conversations, you will then be able to add your new language onto your CV. It is common knowledge that in most English speaking countries around the world, the number of bilingual and multilingual speakers are low compared with most non-English speaking countries. Because of this reason, the ability to speak another language is held in high regard by many employers in English speaking countries as this can be seen as an unusual ability. Even if the language you have learned has no relation to the job you want, being able to speak in another language can still be interesting to a potential new employer as this shows an achievement that needs self motivation and diligence.

There is also a possibility of moving to another country for work purposes for a temporary or permanent basis. If there is a downturn in the economy in your country and you can speak another language, then this gives you extra options for following your career path.

Recent studies show that the UK is losing billions of pounds every year in revenue because companies lack any employees with the ability to speak in another language other than English. A UK poll showed that 15% of people said they could hold a conversation in French, 6% in German and 2% in Italian. I personally believe this figure to actually be lower then what these statistics say as I have met people on occasion who say they speak a particular language; however, when I try to speak with them in one of these languages, I find the reality is they can only say a few sentences in that language. On the other hand, I have met many foreign visitors who come to the UK who say their English is not good, but from the fact that you are stood there having a conversation in English with them proves they can speak good English. This seems to show a point-of-view and maybe cultural difference about language abilities of people in the UK and in other countries.

In 2013, the British council came up with a list of languages they perceive as the top 10 most important languages they would like people in the UK to learn. This list is based on a number of economic, political, cultural and educational factors. They tried to define the list of languages that would be, in their own words, *"will be crucial importance for the UK's prosperity, security and influence in the world over the next 20 years"*. The list is as follows, in order of the most important.

1. Spanish
2. Arabic
3. French
4. Chinese Mandarin
5. German
6. Portuguese
7. Italian
8. Russian
9. Turkish
10. Japanese

Something that may be more interesting to you is the fact that there has been lots of research carried out across the western world showing people who speak more than one language get paid more on average than their mono-lingual counterparts. This even includes cases where the language is not being used in the job.

## Holiday and travelling

Someone who has learned a new language will often find their first real life situation of using their new learned language being on holiday abroad or while traveling abroad. When you first try to speak to another person in their own language when they are not able to speak any English, will give you a great opportunity to test your language skills. If you were able to have any sort of success in the conversation, then you will come away with feelings of achievement. Even if you are someone who has studied a language for a few weeks. This will allow you to engage more with locals and experience things you wouldn't have been able to do otherwise. This will also be the perfect place to practice your language everyday.

## Health Benefits

Learning a second language has a number of health benefits. There have been many studies that show learning a second language can help prevent Alzheimers and dementia. This even includes learning a language later in life. Other than this very important reason, learning a language is a great work out for your brain. I have personally experienced improvements in my memory. This improvement is also backed up by research across the world. This research shows that these same benefits are felt by most people learning extra languages. Other benefits that have been found by various studies include brain growth, improved listening skills, better multi-tasking and increased attention.

## Thinking on a different level

Learning a new language could change how you think about everyday activities and change how you perceive ideas in a very beneficial way. All languages are constructed grammatically in different ways, some more complex than others. This means that you need to think in different ways in order to properly construct meaningful sentences in another language. Saying the same sentence in different languages usually means moving the different grammatical elements to different places. If I take the simple sentence.

*'I will teach him some French'.* In many other languages, these grammatical elements are not in the same place. This sentence could change into *'I him will teach French'* in one language or *'I to him French teach'* in another. In some languages, not all of these words are needed to express this sentence and in other languages more words will be needed for this sentence to make sense that may not have a direct translation in English. These are all reasons why you will need to think differently while speaking in other languages. Why is this beneficial? Because this will allow you to look at the world at a different angle and it will help you to tackle other daily challenges in different ways.

# Grammar and language terms

Before you start learning another language it would be helpful to become familiar with many of the basic language grammar terms. There may be grammar terms listed in this chapter that you are not familiar with. Personally, I didn't have much knowledge of most of the language grammar terms listed in this chapter until I started learning my first foreign language. The following listed grammar terms will probably also appear in your obtained resources and these terms will be explained next to sentence examples in the language you are learning. Because of this, do not feel you need to learn any of these listed rules right now as some of these grammar rules may not be applicable for the language you are learning.

## Noun
A person, place or thing.
*For example: John, England, plane.*

## Pronoun
Words that serve as substitutes for nouns, for the purpose of keeping us from repeating the same noun.
*For example: I, me, you, he, him, she, mine, your.*

## Verb
Action or emotion words that can be (for some languages) conjugated into many tenses of past, present and future.
*For example: to go, to run, to fight, to want*

## Infinitive
A verb before it has been conjugated. For example, the infinitive for 'I am' is 'to be' and the infinitive for 'I cried' is 'to cry'.
*For example: to go, to run, to fight, to want.*

## Tense
This refers to the different states a verb can be in. The present, past, future, conditional are some examples of tenses.
*For example: Infinite - 'to run'.*
*Present tense - I run.*

*Past tense - I ran.*
*Past progressive tense- I was running.*
*Future tense - I will run.*
*Conditional tense - I would run.*
In the English language, we use the word *'will'* in front of a verb to create a future tense and the word *'would'* in front of a verb to create a conditional tense.

## Conjugation
This refers to the different forms of a verb when affected by person, number, gender, tense, aspect, mood, voice, or other grammatical categories.
*For example: I am, he is, you are - These example are conjugations of the verb 'to be'.*

## Preposition
Words that show a noun or pronoun's relationship to another word in the sentence.
*For example: above, below, against, along, near, inside.*

## Conjunction
A word that joins words, phrases and sentences together.
*For example: and, but, or, as much as, even if, unless.*

## Interjection
A word used to express a sudden emotion. Nouns, adjectives, verbs and adverbs can become interjections when they are used as exclamations
*For example: Go! Help! Ah! Alas! Strange!*

## Adjective

Words that describe nouns such as beauty, colour, age, goodness and size. In English, adjectives are always placed before the noun but in some other languages the adjective will be placed after the noun.

*For example: Ugly, yellow, small, old, horrible.*

## Adverb

Words that describe or modify verbs, adjectives or sometimes another adverb.

*For example: Softly, quietly, often, sometimes.*

## Article

A word paired with a noun to show whether the noun is used in a particular or general sense.

*For example: a, an, the.*

## Definite article

In English, this refers to one word, *'the'*. In some other languages there are more than one definite article. In French, the definite articles are *'le' 'la'* or *'les'*, depending on the gender and whether the noun is plural or not. Some languages like Chinese do not use definite articles. A definite article is used to refer to something that in the context of the situation has only one of this thing.

*Example of this would be 'the moon'. If we say 'a moon' then we will be referring to a moon as an example among many moons.*

## Indefinite article

In English we use either the word *'a'* or *'an'* for an indefinite article depending on whether it comes before a noun that starts with a vowel or consonant. Some other languages use more than two indefinite articles and some languages don't use indefinite articles.

*Example of this would be 'a thief stole my things' 'a' is used here because we don't know who the thief is.*

## Reflective verb

We use reflective verbs when we need to refer back to ourselves after the verb.

*For example: I wash myself, I shave myself.*

## Object and subject

Objects and subjects refers to words within many typical sentences. The object refers to the person or thing doing the action, while the subject refers to the person or thing being acted upon. Objects and subjects are normally split by a verb.

*For example: Dave (subject) loves Cricket (object). The police (subject) have caught two people (object).*

## Active vs Passive

A sentence is either active or passive. In an active sentence, the thing doing the action is the subject and the thing receiving the action is the object.

*For example: Lee eats the apple.*

With a passive sentence, the thing receiving the action is

the subject and the thing doing the action is often placed at the end.

*For example: The apple is being eaten by Lee.*

We use the active or passive to change the word emphasis. In the first example Lee is being emphasised and on the second example the apple is being emphasised.

## Imperative

This refers to the command version of a verb.

*For example: Wait!, Go!*

## Phrasal verb

Phrasal verbs are usually two-word phrases consisting of a verb plus an adverb or a verb plus a preposition.

*For example: blow up, ask around, find out.*

## Preposition

These are words that precede nouns and pronouns to form phrases or show relationships among nouns.

*For example: at, by, for, with, from.*

## Gender

Genders exists in English in a limited way. For example, *'actor'* and *'actress'*. In some other languages genders are more important as every noun in these languages are matched with one type of gender. The type of gender used with a noun normally means that other words in that same sentence will also need to follow a change according to which gender type is being used.

## Idiom

An idiom refers to expressions that have developed though some meaning in the past and have stuck as a common way to express a meaning.

*Common English idioms are: 'A piece of cake', 'Let the cat out of the bag', 'Raining cats and dogs', 'Hit the nail on the head'.*

## Formal vs Informal

There are many English words that we would not normally use in conversations with family and friends. These words are more frequently used in literature and in formal speech such as words commonly heard on news reports and formal presentations. Conversely, there are many informal words that are used in daily speech between friends and family that would unlikely be used in formal situations.

*Examples of some formal words: Inconvenience, satisfactory, subsidise.*

*A comparison example: 'incorrect and wrong', 'correct and right', 'purchase and buy'.*

## Particle

A particle is a function word that must be associated with another word or phrase to give meaning. Therefore, particles on their own may not have any meaning.

## Language terms used in this book

Below are a few terms used in this book which might not be familiar to everyone who is reading. As a summary, I've written a brief description for each of these terms below.

### Frequency level

This refers to the amount of times a word occurs naturally in a language though general usage. For example, the word *'the'* will occur many times during written and spoken English, so this word has a very high frequency level. The word 'discombobulate' will rarely appear in written and spoken English so it has a very low frequency rate.

### Polyglot

This word refers to someone who speaks many languages.

### False friend

False friends refer to words that occur in other languages that look and sound the same or similar to words in the English language, but they do not have the same meaning. An example of this would be with the French verb 'Demander'. You would be forgiven to think that this verb means 'to demand' but it means 'to ask for'; therefore, it is a false friend.

### Passive learning

Passive learning refers to learning something without the full attention of the learner.

### Mnemonic

A Mnemonic is your own personal method of remembering something. A common example of a mnemonic would be *'Naughty Elephants Squirt Water'*. Many children including myself, learned this mnemonic at school in order to help us remember the north, east, south and west directions on a compass.

## Keywords

If you see [target language], [language] or [country] used in this book, it should be replaced with the language or country that is relevant to you.

# Learn a language to what level?

The title of this books states that you will be able to speak a new language after 1 year of studying for around 1 hour per day while following the guidance from this book. The question being answered in this chapter is, what level will you reach when this time period is over? It will be a level that you will be able to use to communicate with native speakers face-to-face without the help of English. You will be able to participate in daily conversations and discuss many daily topics. However, you won't reach a fluent level, but this is something you can continue to work on after the year is over, if you choose to do so. I had just used the word *fluent* in the last paragraph and I want to raise a couple of points about the use of this word. The definition of this word raises some arguments among many people as to what language level the word fluent is actually referring to. For me, a fluent level in a language refers to an adult native level or at least a near adult native level. I have read several on-line articles about this topic. Some of these articles say the word fluent refers to a person being able to speak comfortably on a general topic. In which case, if you agree with this definition, you will be fluent after the 365 days of language learning is over using the methods obtained from this book. The definition also seems to change depending on the dictionary you look at. I have one dictionary that states the definition of fluent is 'Able to speak or write a particular foreign language easily and accurately' and another that says 'When a person is fluent, they can speak a language easily, well, and quickly'. It's difficult to get a real idea of the level from these short explanations. I don't however believe that being fluent in a language means you will be 100% perfect in that language. I remember first going to university and learning many new English words that I didn't know before attending as well as needing to improve aspects of my English grammar in order to write my 12,000 word dissertation. Was I not fluent before going to college? I still make English grammar mistakes now on occasion and for this reason, I have a book on my desk with the title 'Quick solutions to common errors in English' by Angela Burt.

It is difficult to define levels in a language. What one person perceives as advanced another person will say the level is only intermediate. English speaking counties normally refer to the following level terms: novice, beginner, lower intermediate, intermediate, upper intermediate, advanced, and fluent. From these terms it is not easy to judge what level a person is at any one stage. In other parts of Europe many people including the professional world of languages have adopted the Common European Framework of reference for languages with the acronym CEFR. This system tries to define your level based on a written description for each of the levels. From beginner to fluent, the levels go in the following order. A1, A2, B1, B2, C1, C2. There are many on-line tests for many languages that you can use to test your level based on the following criteria.

**The descriptions of these levels by CEFR are as follows:**

## A1

Can understand and use familiar everyday expressions and very basic phrases aimed at the satisfaction of needs of a concrete type. Can introduce him/herself and others and can ask and answer questions about personal details such as where he/she lives, people he/she knows and things he/she has. Can interact in a simple way provided the other person talks slowly and clearly and is prepared to help.

## A2

Can understand sentences and frequently used expressions related to areas of most immediate relevance (e.g. very basic personal and family information, shopping, local geography, employment). Can communicate in simple and routine tasks requiring a simple and direct exchange of information on familiar and routine matters. Can describe in simple terms aspects of his/her background, immediate environment and matters in areas of immediate need.

## B1

Can understand the main points of clear standard input on familiar matters regularly encountered in work, school, leisure, etc. Can deal with most situations likely to arise whilst travelling in an area where the language is spoken. Can produce simple connected text on topics which are familiar or of personal interest. Can describe experiences and events, dreams, hopes and ambitions and briefly give reasons and explanations for opinions and plans.

## B2

Can understand the main ideas of complex text on both concrete and abstract topics, including technical discussions in his/her field of specialisation. Can interact with a degree of fluency and spontaneity that makes regular interaction with native speakers quite possible without strain for either party. Can produce clear, detailed text on a wide range of subjects and explain a viewpoint on a topical issue giving the advantages and disadvantages of various options.

## C1

Can understand a wide range of demanding, longer texts, and recognise implicit meaning. Can express him/herself fluently and spontaneously without much obvious searching for expressions. Can use language flexibly and effectively for social, academic and professional purposes. Can produce clear, well-structured, detailed text on complex subjects, showing controlled use of organisational patterns, connectors and cohesive devices.

## C2

Can understand with ease virtually everything heard or read. Can summarise information from different spoken and written sources, reconstructing arguments and accounts in a coherent presentation. Can express him/herself spontaneously, very fluently and precisely, differentiating finer shades of meaning even in the most complex situations.

In my opinion, from reading these descriptions, there is a very large jump in required ability between B1, B2 and C1 which is also the levels that most people will find the most difficult and slowest point to progress in a language. I believe you shouldn't pay too much attention to these level terms as you will know your own level from your ability to communicate effectively with others. It is common to be asked while in a conversation what level you are in a language and I very often hear the CEFR reference being mentioned. If this happens to you while in a language exchange, you will now know what others are referring to.

The language level that you will reach after following this book for a year will vary depending on many different factors. The amount of time you are able to spend per day studying your language is one of the most important factors. If you spend an hour and a half per day learning a language then you are going to be learning twice as fast as someone learning only for 45 minutes per day. I recommend spending around an hour a day studying your new language but if you can spend more time studying then this will be better. Do not study for too many hours in one single day as this could burn you out and it could drain your motivation. It could lead to you to quitting the language all together. Learning a little everyday will help to keep your motivation and interest high in the language. The language you have chosen is also a major factor that is going to make a big difference to your final language level as languages have different difficulty levels. As well as this, the number of resources, the number of native speakers available to speak with, the type of alphabet the language uses and if this is your first foreign language are extra factors that will determine the level you are going to reach. However, if you follow the advice in this book and spend the time learning your new language for 365 consecutive days, then you will reach a good conversational level.

# My own experience of learning languages

I don't remember having any thoughts about wanting to learn another language from when I was a young child. Maybe the idea of learning another language felt like an unachievable goal at a young age or maybe I was just too interested in other normal child things. My father is a French citizen and speaks French as well as English. As a young child I remember being fascinated with the French language. I was often asking my father how to say everyday objects in French. I also remember visiting my family in France at a young age and not being able to communicate with them as most of them didn't speak English.

As a child I went to a standard comprehensive school in the city of Bristol in England, where I was also raised. I started secondary school there in 1991. When we began our first year in secondary school we started our first mandatory language lessons. The two languages that were taught at my school at that time were French and German. These two languages were the typical two languages that were also taught in almost every school. Since 2008, schools in England now have a greater flexibility to choose almost any language they want; as a result of this, many schools have made efforts to introduce new languages. The language that has been adopted by most schools is Spanish, but there are many schools teaching other new languages. At my school, I was given 2 years of German classes and 3 years of French classes. In the 3 years of learning French, my French language teacher never said anything in the French language to us. I remember having to read out French sentences in my class with the task of pronouncing words correctly, but I was never getting corrected by the teacher. Lessons normally consisted of simple and unnecessary vocabulary and sentence repetition. By the end of the 3 years of French and 2 years of German I could only say a few fixed sentences in these two languages. I had spent 5 years of my life studying these languages, but I had not reached a level even close to a conversational level in either French or German. It is now, after studying languages on my own and trying different language learning methods that I realise the reason for my lack of success was not only due to my lack of effort in the classroom but it was also due to the methods used in the classroom to teach us the languages. This problem is not only unique to schools but also a problem in many language learning courses in collages and universities, who tend to use similar teaching methods of vocabulary and grammar building.

After finishing comprehensive school, I passed five years at college and university learning Graphic design. When I reached my forth year in higher education I decided to take the challenge of learning French by myself. I went to my local book shop and I bought a book called, 'Learn French in 6 weeks'. And yes, I actually thought this book was going to teach me to speak conversational French in 6 weeks. I followed the course very closely everyday and after 6 weeks to my surprise, I was not able to speak French in any sort of useful way. I could only say some very basic sentences. This 6 week course included no audio, as a result, what I thought I could say was prob-ably pronounced incorrectly anyway. It seems crazy to me now that I had ever thought this book would help me to speak conversationally in the French language, but I had the willingness to learn, and so I continued trying to learn French on and off in my spare time while I was not stud-ying at university or later on, working. I carried on doing this for several years, using similar methods to what I had used at school. This included lots of vocabulary repeti-tion and lots of grammar exercises. During some years my French either showed no improvement or even seemed to get worse. The only reason preventing me from quitting, was the fact that I had already spent a long time learning French. I didn't want to have all that time spent learning French wasted for nothing. I decided to look more into the way I was actually learning. I started to research other language learning methods. I found to my surprise that people on the YouTube video website showing off their language abilities by speaking many different languages. Sometimes even more than 10 languages. It was at this point when I thought that the methods I was currently using were probably not the best, and that I must find a different learning approach. I looked at different methods to learn vocabulary and grammar as well as looking into methods to improve my speaking and reading ability. I researched topics such as how we remember new words and how we retain our memories. I continued to make changes until I started to improve my learning progress at a faster rate than before. I then found myself reaching a level where I could communicate with native speakers. I knew I was making improvements as I was noticing the improvements from month to month. I also now realise that noticing these improvements is an important part of learning anything as it allows you to customise your learning process. If you feel that during a period of time there have been no improvements in your language ability, then you can make adjustments to your learning methods. I hope to have done most of this work for you, as the guidance in this book will keep you from using poor learning methods and resources.

I continued to change my methods until a time came when I was comfortable speaking French. I was surprised at the rate I was able to learn French once I had finally discovered how to learn a language more effectively. I wanted to continue the experience, so I decided to try to learn Spanish using the same methods that helped me to successfully learn French. It was a slow start as I had to research into better methods for a beginning language learner. From my research and from trail and error I realised that the different stages of language learning required different methods. After only 6 months of learning Spanish for 1 hour a day, I was able to join in basic conversations with native Spanish speakers. After 8 months I had moved to more intermediate conversations involving different topics. After 1 year I was able to understand lots of normal rate Spanish speech and I made a big improvement with my grammar. I had reached a point in the language that I was happy with and to this day I am able to join in with many Spanish conversations. After Spanish, I decided to give myself a more difficult challenge. I decided to try learning Chinese Mandarin. This language definitely had a more difficult learning curve. I had to do more research into better ways to learn this very different language. In the first 6 months of learning Chinese Mandarin, I did not see the same progress as I had made while studying Spanish, consequently I made further changes to my learning until I was able to start to make conversations with Chinese people a regular thing. I have now also reached a good level of Chinese Mandarin that allows me to communicate with native Chinese people. I have since travelled to China twice and I have used my Chinese Mandarin language in more than 10 cities around China. On my second trip to china I decided I would try to travel to another Asian country while I was there, so as a new year's resolution as well as being at a point in time that coincided with me starting to write this book. I started to learn the Thai language. I learned Thai almost everyday for 8 months until my arrival. I had good success with this difficult language proving to myself that the techniques described in this book work.

I would also like to continue to learn more languages. Some languages that currently interest me and that I have both looked into as well as considered studying full time in the future are, Italian, Romanian, Persian, Vietnamese and Japanese.

# Language choice

There are an estimated 7000 languages being spoken around the world of which you are going take on the challenge of learning one of these languages. The fact that you are reading this book means it is likely you have already chosen a language to learn, or at least you have an idea from a number of different languages you would like to choose from. Your decision on which language you chose to learn will determine how fast you will progress. There are many different reasons for this; the obvious one being that all languages have different difficulty levels. The difficulty level of a language is mainly determined by how different the language is from your own language; or if you already speak 2 or 3 languages, then the difference between the language you want to learn compared with all the languages you currently speak. These differences includes grammar, word order, vocabulary, pronunciation and the language's alphabet. If the language you have chosen to learn uses a Roman alphabet like the English alphabet then this is going to help in the language learning process as you are not going to need to learn another alphabet and most of the characters in a Roman alphabet will probably have many similar sounding pronunciations. Other factors that will make a language more difficult is the number of resources available for that language. I have seen reports showing the language learning business to be a multi-billion pound business. This in turn, means there are many companies in the world trying to take their cut of this money by producing resources for language learners to purchase. The large number of different companies involved means there is lots of competition. This is a good thing for us, the consumer, because when there is competition, it results in cheaper prices and increased resource quality. However, I have had experience of purchasing resources that have been poor in quality and there are many resources available that charge a high price for what you actually get in return. In a later chapter, I will give you suggestions for the types of resources you should be looking for as well as a number of specific resource recommendations that I have found useful for my language learning.

The companies who produce the language learning

resources naturally choose to provide resources covering languages that are most popular with the language learning public in order to gain maximum profit. The 4 main languages that I most often see being included (not including English) are Spanish, French, Italian and German. As a part of a second less frequently seen group we can include Portuguese, Chinese Mandarin, Japanese, Russian and Arabic. If we go down further to another group again, we can include Dutch, Swedish, Persian, Romanian, Indonesian, Thai, Greek and Korean. Even after this list there are still plenty of resources for many other lesser well known languages. However, if you wanted to learn a very obscure language, for example, Tongan; derived from the country Tonga. Then it's going to be much more difficult to learn this language compared with French or Spanish, simply because you will have far less learning resources at your disposal. The good news is, if you want to learn any of the languages in the list featured above or in the lists featured in the 'why learn a language' chapter then there will be a high number of good quality resources for you to choose from.

At some point, you are going to need to start to practice speaking your new language; therefore, you need to be able to practice speaking with native speakers of that language. Luckily for us, there are many people around the world learning English, as English is seen as the most important language to learn by many countries. Because of this reason, it is normally easy to find native speakers to practice your language with for most languages. The number of available native speakers to speak with is yet another factor that determines the difficultly level of a language, as having language partners available to speak with is a vital part of learning a language that you need to have access to. You won't just need to have one language partner. You will need to find as many people as you can to practice with. This includes males and females, because with some languages, grammar and vocabulary can change depending if a male or female is speaking. I reviewed all of the different applications that I normally use to find language partners over several days and over different time periods. From this review I have created the list below in order of how easy it was for me to find people to practice my language with.

**In order of how easy it was to find a language partner:**

1. Spanish
2. Portuguese
3. Chinese mandarin
4. Arabic
5. French
6. Russian
7. Italian
8. Korean
9. German
10. Japanese

In a later chapter I will list the many different websites that I use to find native speakers to practice my languages.

It's healthy for your motivation in learning a language to have reasons to learn a language. Apart from learning French, which allowed me to communicate with my French family, I didn't have a specific reason to learn my other languages. The pleasure of learning and being able to speak with interesting new people was reason enough for me. Some reasons for learning a language that I have heard from other people include:

- Having family members from another country.
- Travelled on holiday to another country and enjoyed it so much they now want to learn that language.
- Important for a job.
- Planning on moving to a different country.
- Interested in a culture.
- Wanting to set their self a challenge.

Today's languages are derived from older languages that have been mixed together over thousands of years through mass migrations and wars, meaning there are many languages that have similarities to each other because they share the same language ancestors. This commonality could be a number things including grammar, vocabulary, pronunciation and/or spelling. When you have success-fully learned one language from a language group, then the other languages from that same group are going to be easier to learn. For example, if you learn one of the romance languages: French, Spanish, Italian, Portuguese, Catalan or Romanian, then learning an additional romance language will be easier. If you look at related languages to English, then often the languages: Dutch, Frisian and German (more specifically Low German) are referred to as being the most closely related languages to English but the differences are still great enough that often French and Spanish are still considered to be easier languages to learn for an English speaker.

If you are unsure which language you want to learn and you don't have any major reason to learn any particular language or you would simply like to challenge yourself at learning a language then I would highly recommend Spanish. Spanish is not only the easiest natural language to learn in many aspects (not including man made languages such as Esperanto), it also has the most resources, the highest number of available speakers to practice with and it is a very useful language to learn as there are many Spanish speaking countries in the world.

To help you to decide, there are a number of useful websites available on the internet to get language over-views. I have listed some of these websites below that you can use to find out more information.

- www.how-to-learn-any-language.com
- www.omniglot.com
- www.freelanguage.org
- www.about.com/education/
- www.bbc.co.uk/languages/

# The language learning curve

The graph shown in this chapter depicts the typical learning curve for language learning. The curve will change a little from language to language depending on many different language factors, but overall the learning curve will still hold this similar shape. Generally, at the beginning of learning anything, you pick up the basics easily, because your confidence and self motivation is high at taking on this new challenge; therefore, in a short space of time you will have gone from having no knowledge to being able to do something that most other people cannot do. When you divide a big task into chunks, we normally take on the easier tasks to begin with. Because of this, the perception is you are making good progress from the start. This generally happens for a few months until you hit the upper beginner level. Even though you are still learning lots of new things at this level, you start to tackle the more trickier words and grammar rules as well as having to recap on some of the earlier rules and words you started learning at the beginning. This means your perceived learning progress slows down and everything starts to feel more difficult than before. This feeling will last throughout the intermediate stages and it is during this time that you must have the motivation to continue learning your new language as you will notice less improvements throughout this time period even though you are taking in just as much information as before. This feeling is normal, but it is very important to keep learning everyday and put aside any feelings of quitting. If you continue with the learning methods as described in this book, you will get past this intermediate level and you will arrive at a point when the learning process begins to feel quicker again. This generally indicates that you have arrived at an upper intermediate level. I believe the learning process starts to feel easier at this level because many of the different factors from the language you are learning starts to connect with each other and sentences start to make more sense. Learning at this point becomes more enjoyable as you start using more of your time to take part in conversations with native speakers. At the more advanced stages, you will make quicker progress with the language until you reach a point where improvements can no longer be made from using books. You will only be able to improve your language level further by actually taking part in many conversations as this allows you to come across all of the finer details in a language such as colloquial expressions, idioms and slang words.

## Typical learning curve

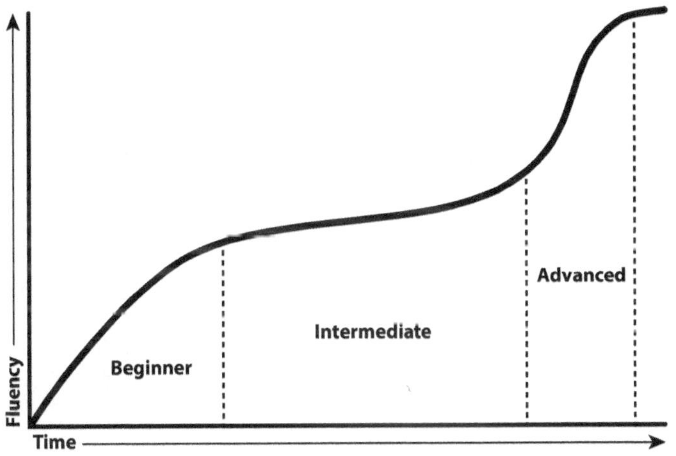

# Language learning secrets

## Grammar

I have myself experienced a long period of time of self study with all my efforts placed on learning vocabulary and grammar. I found this process slow, difficult, mentally draining and it was not an enjoyable experience. Spending too much time learning grammar was hindering my chances of ever successfully learning a language and it was at the very least slowing the process down and making the experience unpleasant. I started to move away from prioritising grammar in my language learning after reading articles from several experienced language learners who were saying that studying grammar is not as important in language learning compared with other language learning aspects. At first, my thoughts were something like *"this can't be true, you need grammar to know how to combine all the words together"* and you may be thinking the same as I did. My thoughts at the time were also *"this is the way we were taught at school, so it must be correct"*. Now that I have experienced learning a language from a beginner to a conversational level without placing much emphasis on studying grammar, I now realise that studying grammar is indeed less important to successfully learn a language than I had previously believed. I'm not saying that you should forget about studying grammar all together, I'm saying that you should put the importance of studying grammar behind other aspects of language learning. We still need to learn grammar but we can learn grammar using a more natural method by speaking and reading the language while our brains make the connections in the language. This is similar to how a child learns a language. I still think it is a good idea to own a grammar book. A grammar book is a useful tool to have as a reference book, to have ready when you want to look up a particular grammar rule that you are currently having a difficult time working out how to use correctly.

While learning my first foreign language, I purchased a grammar book and I started learning grammar from first page until the last page. This method did not work well for me. By studying too much grammar from an early stage had meant that I found myself thinking too much about all the different grammar rules while I was trying to speak and think in the language. This caused me to talk at a slow awkward pace and ironically I was making more grammar mistakes than I would have otherwise. You will find that by learning grammar naturally as you progress through reading and speaking will help you to remember grammar rules easier.

There are, however, several basic grammar concepts useful to learn early on in the language learning process. Apart from obvious grammar aspects such as word order, negation and verb tenses, which are normally better learned through context. I find that it is helpful to get an understanding of the following grammar points listed below, so that you are ready to use them by the time you start practicing your speaking. Because of this, it would be useful to get a good grasp of how these grammar points work within the first 3 months of learning your new language.

## 1. Making comparisons

I make comparisons many times during conversations with my language partners. I will use sentences such as; *'I speak better French now than I did before'*, or *'I think French is more difficult than Spanish'*. You should know how to say; *'A compared to B is better/cheaper/bigger/smaller'* or another way we better express this in English is *'A is better/cheaper/ bigger/smaller than B'*. Some languages have different ways to express this idea, so you need to find out how to make comparisons correctly in the language you are learning. Another comparison sentence example that would be helpful for you to learn is *'A and B are similar/very different/ the same'*.

## 2. Before and After

In the English language, the two words 'before' and 'after' are high frequency words. The first step is to learn how to say them in your new language. Then, you need to learn how to use them correctly. Examples of their usage in English would be *'after I graduate, I will move to Brazil'* and *'before I eat my dinner I will speak to my friend'*. For some languages, the grammar works in the same way as English, but for some other languages the grammar rules for using these two words are different, meaning that the placement of these words could be placed at different parts of the sentence.

## 3. Indefinite plurals

You shouldn't let the name indefinite plurals put you off as this is a simple piece of grammar that is useful to learn in the early stages. It is basically a way of expressing an unspecified number or an amount attached to a noun. We can take the noun 'books' and use it for some examples: *'a lot of books', 'a few books', 'many books', 'some books'* etc. Learning both the vocabulary for these indefinite plurals and how these indefinite plurals are attached to a noun is something you will be using often.

## 4. Time expressions

When I start speaking in a new language I find I am often having to use time expressions because in early conversation, topics often consist of talking about: when you started learning the language, how long you have been learning the language, when you will next practice, how often you learn the language etc. Because of this, I find it very useful to learn many time expressions from an early stage. It is useful to learn how to say the following phrases and it is also useful to learn how they fit within a typical sentence:

- in 10 days time
- 10 days ago
- last week/last time
- next week/next time
- sometimes, often, not often, always, from time to time, once in a while.

## 5. Question words and types of questions

Knowing how to say the seven question words: who, where, when, why, what, which and how is very useful in both being able to ask questions and being able to notice when questions are being asked by others. You will not only need to know how to say these words but you will also need to know how questions are formed in the language you are learning. Most languages have multiple ways to ask questions just as we do in the English language.

## Pronunciation

Pronunciation can fall into two categories. One aspect of learning pronunciation in a language is the need to pronounce words correctly based on the pronunciation rules of that language. Another aspect of pronunciation is changing your pronunciation to have an accent similar to a native speaker of that language. It is possible that you will be able to naturally improve your accent close to an authentic level while you are learning, but the main focus of this book is correcting your pronunciation in order to simply be understood. Your first task in learning a language will be to learn how to pronounce the different characters and combinations of characters from the language's alphabet. Characters may also change their pronunciation when placed at different parts of a word as some languages have irregular sounds that you will need to memorise. When you begin your language learning, you should start this process by listening to all of the sounds from the language while linking these sounds together with each of the characters. As you start reading dialogues from your resources you will remember some of the sounds and you will forget others, this is normal. A mistake would be to spend lots of time mastering the pronunciation of a language before even starting to learn any actual content. If you are still making pronunciation mistakes after 5 or 6 months; then, this isn't generally going to be a problem as you are probably still going to be understood most of the time. Three pronunciation challenges that you may come across are:

1.  Characters or combinations of characters that have no equivalent sound in English.
2.  Inconsistent sounds across different words.
3.  Languages that don't use the Roman alphabet.

We can take Spanish as an example for challenge number 1. Most sounds in Spanish are either the same or similar to English, but there are a few exceptions that have completely different sounds. One of these exceptions is with the 'rr' sound. This requires a lot of practice to pronounce correctly; however, it isn't necessary to pronounce the 'rr' correctly to be understood by a Spanish speaker. If you pronounce it similar to a long English 'r', then you will still be understood. Now we will look at the Chinese Mandarin language, as this language contains lots of new sounds that differ from English that will need to be learned. Unfortunately pronouncing many of these sounds incorrectly will mean you generally won't be understood. Therefore you will need to do more listening and pronunciation practice for this language. You will need to move your tongue and mouth into new positions until you are able to produce the new sounds. Chinese Mandarin is also an example of a language that contains sounds that are very similar to each other, as a result, as a beginner learning Chinese Mandarin you may first think many of these sounds are the same. It would only be after a few months of listening to these sounds before the language learner would start to distinguish the different sounds apart from each other. This process can feel quite frustrating when native speakers of the language you are learning initially don't understand what you are saying, but if you continue to practice a little everyday, then you will find that this is a learning curve bump that you can soon get over.

The second pronunciation problem that I had listed was languages that do not have consistent sounding letters or combination of letters across different words. This is actually a common complaint with people learning our own English language. English is an inconsistently pronounced language. There are many examples of words that sound the same but are spelt differently. Examples of these are 'no/know', 'to/too/two', 'mail/male', 'plain/plane' etc. There are also many words that are spelt the same but are pronounced differently depending on the meaning of that word. The grammar term for this is homograph. Examples of this are polish, minute, record, wind etc. We can take the two languages, French and Spanish as examples, as they are closely related languages but have very different pronunciation rules. Spanish is a consistently pronounced language, but French has completely different pronunciation rules and has many pronunciation inconsistencies. This makes the French language more difficult to learn for a language learning beginner.

The final challenge has to do with the language's alphabet. Many languages do not use the romanised alphabet that we are all accustomed with in English. The benefit of learning a language with a romanised alphabet is that many of the characters will normally either have the same sound or at least will have a similar sound compared with the English

Alphabet. Because of this, you will learn the pronunciation of a language quicker with a romanised alphabet as you will be able to recognise the sounds easier by looking at the characters. If you have chosen a language that does not use the romanised alphabet, then this will raise the challenge of having to learn the sounds of each and every new character; therefore, you should start by using the language's standardised romanised phonetic system if the language you are learning has one. This would be the next best thing.

## Vocabulary

When I started to learn French, I put a lot of effort into learning new words. I was trying to learn almost every new word that I had come across. My thinking at the time was – I was going to be able to commit all of these new words to memory by repeatedly learning each word and then I would be able to recall these words when needed, whilst using the grammar that I was also learning to put the different words together. I thought I could put these two elements together and one day become fluent. My daily learning method consisted of learning some grammar from one of the few grammar books that I had purchased and then I would learn some vocabulary from a list of new words that I have accumulated. I unfortunately continued using this method over several years, after which, I spoke very little French, comparable to someone from a beginner level. I was also learning the wrong sorts of words as well as learning these words with ineffective methods compared to methods I would use today.

In order to reach a conversational level in another language you will need to learn a smaller amount of words than most people think they would need. Research shows that for most languages, by learning 20% of the most frequent words in a language will make up about 80% of the words used in average daily conversations. The new words that you will be purposely learning during this 1 year challenge should therefore be high frequency words while the remaining lower frequency words will be learned gradually and naturally as you are studying the language from reading, writing and speaking. People's ideas about learning new words stems partly from education institutes, as students are taught to remember unnecessary lists of words that are not needed in the early stages. The sorts of vocabulary lists I remember learning at school and I often see in some beginner language learning books are lists of: fruits, vegetables, animals, body parts, foods, clothes, musical instruments, parts of a car, items in a house and many other similar types of lists. These groups of words are unlikely to appear regularly in a daily conversation at even an intermediate level. It's a good idea to learn a few of the obvious key words that tend to appear often in many of the learning materials such as: cat, dog, apple, head, table, t-shirt etc. You will know when to add particular words to your vocabulary list when they start to regularly appear in your language learning materials or when you feel you need a particular word during a language exchange. As a beginner, you only need to purposely learn words that will be useful while having an informal conversation about a general topic, as these are the types of conversations that you will often be taking part in.

There will be times when you remember new words naturally without even trying to. I find this is often due to a word being in some way similar to the English equivalent. Maybe the word is borrowed from the English language or over history the foreign word had made it into the English language, because of this, the word may sound similar. Maybe the word has some other personal link that allows you to remember it more easily, such as the sound of a person's name who is close to you or maybe the name of your pet. This all helps to create a visual clue for remembering new words and you should try to take advantage of this when possible.

Most languages have formal and informal words for expressing a meaning. Some examples in our English language of informal and formal words are *find out/ discover*, *leave out/omit*, *let/permit*, *set up/establish* as well as hundreds of more examples. In the early stages of learning your new language you should ignore almost all formal words as these will unlikely be of any use to you in most conversations you are going to have. This is good news for you as this will decrease the number of words you will need to learn. If you discover that a new word you have learned is formal, then try to find an informal version of that meaning and then discard the formal version of this word. I have found that in general, when having conversations with native speakers, they almost always speak using only informal words. The only reason you may want to purposely learn formal words would be if you are learning your new language for work purposes or for some other formal occasion.

The goal of learning new words is being able to recall these words from memory when needed, quickly and accurately. This means trying to get new useful words into your long term memory. I did research on memory while learning my languages in an effort to be a more efficient language learner. I discovered that apparently the main problem we face is being able to remember new words, because research shows that remembering new things for the long term is not something we can do consciously. We cannot tell our brains to add words into our long term memory like moving files from folder to folder on a computer. Research shows that if we make an effort to remember a word then we will on most occasions create a memory of this word in only our short term memory. In order to get a word into our long term memory the brain needs to believe it will need the memory of this word for some importance in the future. Short term memory is thought to last around 10 to 14 days and the amount of information your short term memory can hold is limited. This is why it is important for children to revise as much as they can a week before any exams. They need to fill up their short term memory. Therefore, a poor performing student could be able to outscore a high performing student by revising more. Long term memory on the other hand seems to have almost no limit as far as research shows. It's thought the brain has evolved to add only memories of importance to the long term memory that will help in the survival of that person. There is a rare medical condition called Hyperthymesia where the person remembers everything everyday into his or her long term memory. This condition has been shown to have a more detrimental effects than positive; therefore, this may show why our brains are selective on thoughts we remember. We need to try to trick our brains into remembering more of the things we want rather than only need. I find that one of the best methods for getting a word into my long term memory is to use that word naturally in a conversation. We can do this with lots of words at the same time by placing a vocabulary list of words that you are learning in front of you while you are practicing your speaking, this way you can quickly recall words you are learning and then use them naturally in a conversation. You will also need to revise the words from your list using one of the many flashcard applications available on the internet. Once you have added some words to your flashcard application, you should aim to review these words each day using spaced repetition. Spaced repetition refers to the act of prioritising words into different categories depending on how easily you remember a word. This will allow you to revise the words that you most often forget, rather than having to revise every word every day. This will save you time and more importantly it will give you a better chance of remembering the words that you are currently having problems remembering. Many flashcard applications that take advantage of spaced repetition will give you several options for each of the flashcards you review. For example, these options could be 'easy', 'normal' and 'difficult'. It would then be your decision to choose one of these options depending on how easily you have remembered that word. The option you choose will determine the amount of time before you are shown this card again. I talk more about flashcards and vocabulary lists in part 2 of this book.

As I had stated earlier in this chapter, when I first started to learn French I only used vocabulary lists and grammar books. My method for learning new words at that time was to cover up long lists of words and repeatedly test myself until I was able to recall these words before they were uncovered. By using this method I was able to only recall words in isolation as I was learning them without context. I still use vocabulary lists in my language learning today, but the words used in the lists are carefully chosen and learnt together with dialogues; therefore, the meaning of these words are reinforced by context. Learning new words through dialogues will help you to better define the meaning of a word as well as being able to know how to use these words correctly.

We have lots of different personal ways we remember everyday things. The different types of memory we possess are visual, smell, taste, hearing, and muscle memory. If the word you want to learn is an object, you can help yourself by picturing that object in your minds eyes. To demonstrate the effectiveness of this idea, say out aloud the colour of the front door of your house without looking at it... Once you have done this, think back to the process you used before you had remembered this colour. You will find that you will have placed a picture of your door in your mind's eye. This demonstrates the memory link with visual elements.

I want to briefly raise the issue here of verb conjugations and tenses. Some languages don't have verb conjugations and tenses, some languages like English have only a few changes between the different tenses and conjugations, then there are the third set of languages that have many different and varied changes. Verbs are very difficult to visualise because they are not objects. They are actions, therefore they must be learned through context while speaking and reading. I also talk more about learning verbs in part 2 of this book.

If you want to find the highest frequent words in a language, then you can do this by searching on the internet for 'frequency lists' followed by the language you are learning. From this search you should be able to find frequency list website links for many different languages. I don't often use these lists myself, but I have sometimes viewed them in order to pick out a few useful words to add to my vocabulary list.

## Speaking

Speaking your new language with other people is *the* most important factor for improving your language ability. You need to repeatedly practice your speaking in order to improve your language ability in the quickest way, so you need to start speaking as soon as you can. When you start to practice speaking in your new language you will be saying similar words and phrases over and over again as your vocabulary and understanding of the language will be limited. From the very start, you will be building up your vocabulary and sentences in preparation to start speaking your new language. Below is a list of common sentences that I often use in language conversations at an early level. You could learn them in your chosen language before you start speaking. You can use the Google translate website (translate.google.co.uk) to translate each of the following sentences into the language you are learning:

- How are you?
- Can you hear me clearly?
- We don't have a good connection.
- Which country are you from?
- What is your name?
- Which city are you from?
- I'm from [country].
- Can you please repeat?
- Sorry, I don't understand.
- What time is it in your country?
- Can you speak more slowly?
- Recently I have learnt these new words...
- How is your English going?
- How long have you been learning English?
- I've been learning [language] for [number] months.
- Your English level is very good.

- I'm happy with my progress.
- Have you been to [country]?
- How do you say [word] in [language]?
- I work as a [job].
- Are you a student or do you work?
- What is your job?
- What subject are you studying?
- Can you speak any other languages?
- It has been great to meet you.
- Thank you for speaking to me in [language].
- I must now go.
- I must now go to sleep.
- Please add me to Skype.
- My account name is...
- See you again.
- Can you write the meaning for me please?
- I have made a mistake.
- I plan on travelling to your country.
- I'm only joking.
- Let me think...

Knowing these basic sentences will help you to get started in many conversations. When I use the words and sentences that I am learning in a language exchange, I find that these words are more easily remembered the next time I try to recall them. I believe this is because when we use a new word in a conversation, your brain recognises that you are using this word in a natural way and usually adds this information to your long term memory as it considers this information could be important for you in the future.

As you progress through the different stages of learning, the time you spend speaking will increase until the main part of your study is taken up by having conversations in your new language. At this stage, learning becomes less of an effort, because you can start to learn new grammar rules and new words while meeting new interesting people from around the world. There are many useful resources to find language partners. I will list these in the next chapter of this book.

In the early stages of speaking, it is useful to learn some conversation fillers and connectors. This will help your speech sound more natural, less hesitant and you will not have to keep falling back on ummmmm and ahhhhh. These sorts of new words will give you time to think about what your next sentence is going to be. Below is a list of useful conversation connectors and fillers. You will again need to use your dictionary in order to find the equivalent meaning in the language you are learning.

**Conversation connectors:**
- Therefore...
- Futhermore...
- Moreover...
- In fact...
- Actually...
- Basically...
- However...
- Meanwhile...

- For example...
- In order to...
- Regarding...

**Conversation fillers:**
- Let me think...
- In my opinion...
- How do I put this...
- By the way...
- To be honest...
- Come to think of it...
- It depends.
- I agree.
- I see.
- You see...
- You know...
- I mean...
- I guess...
- I imagine...
- Perhaps.
- Maybe.
- Well.
- Fortunately/unfortunately...

As you reach the intermediate stages, you are going to want to discuss other topics in order to help you to build up your vocabulary. Below is a list of topics that I normally use while speaking;
- Reasons for learning languages.

- What have been the difficulties with learning the language.
- Different methods of learning your language.
- About your country and culture.
- The weather and what the weather is normally like.
- Your current job and past jobs.
- Your future plans of travel.
- Places you have travelled.
- Your current and past hobbies.
- About your family.
- Your favourite sports.
- List the words you have been learning that week.
- Talk about what you normally do everyday.
- Talk about what you have been doing this week.

Part 2 of this book will talk more about taking part in language exchanges and I give you more tips on how to benefit most out of your speaking practice.

## Finding time to learn

People have said to me, *"I would love to learn a language but I don't have the free time needed to study"*. In fact, responses back from an on-line questionnaire shows that 'Not enough time' is the number 1 excuse for people not learning a new language even though they would like to do so. The results from this survey are as follows:

- Not enough time - **24%**
- Not able to keep up the motivation - **16%**

- Bad teaching method - 15%
- No access to native speakers - 15%
- Not enough money - 11%
- Worrying about speaking to native speakers - 11%
- No or limited access to good learning material - 5%
- Bad teacher - 3%

All of the points featured in this list are discussed at some point in this book, but for now I want to discuss the number one complaint on this list. Let's say you sleep for 8 hours + work/study for 8 hours + driving 1 hour + eating 1 hour. 24 hours minus this time equates to having 6 hours remaining. Now we just need to take 1 more of these hours out and you can have the rest of this time to do whatever you want. I'm also assuming that you work or study at university around 5 days a week, so you will also have more time on your non-working/non-study days for your language study. I myself work full time, I have a social life, I regularly go to gym and I have other hobbies besides learning languages. I have learned how to fill my free time with language learning. In order to become a successful language learner you need to study your new language at least a little everyday. Once you are able to find the time that you can take for the purposes of studying everyday then you will soon get into a habit of learning.

When is it a good time to study? If possible I would recommend breaking this time up into smaller chunks of time throughout the day. You could wake up early for work to read or practice speaking for 15 to 30 minutes. Your concentration levels are at the highest in the morning, so this would be a great habit to get in to, even if you do this for 1 or 2 days per week. It's also helpful to study your language in the morning if you are looking to speak with native speakers who are in a completely different time zone to you. If you drive a vehicle or use public transport to work or to college/university then I recommend that you listen to language learning content that matches your level whilst travelling, using either your car stereo or with an MP3 player. If your travel to work takes 30 minutes, then this time will total 1 hour per day. 5 hours per week. 275 hours per year. That totals 275 hours that could be classed as dead time. Once you get home from work or study, try to find more time to study your language. If you normally read while in bed then try reading something in the language you are learning.

Some people reading this book may have small children or may have other sorts of responsibilities that keep them from having more time for themselves. At the time of writing, I do not have any children, so it would be wrong for me to question the time parents have to learn a new language. I can only say that if you want to learn a new language badly enough then you need to really look at parts of the day that you can take for yourself for language learning purposes.

## Motivation

After you have begun learning your new language, you will come across days when you will feel like giving up. You will feel like you can't be bothered reading or listening to anything else in the language. You will probably also experience periods of time with the feeling of not having made any improvements in your new language as there are stages in the language learning process that become more difficult to judge whether you are making improvements. There are several techniques I use to keep me motivated that I want to share with you here in case you find yourself in this situation. Most language learners will come across these feelings, but you will often find your feelings change within a few days as long as you persist in learning your language everyday without giving up. Lack of motivation or desire to continue from time to time is normal in any long term task that you take in life. I have come up with my own motivation boasters for learning new languages. I have also tried and tested many ideas from other people around the world who publish their ideas about this openly. Below are some of the motivation methods that I use to prevent me from quitting any long term challenge I take up:

1. Think about how you will feel once you have finally learned the new language. Think about what you would do and what you would be saying.

2. Go back over earlier learning material that you used at the beginning stages of your learning to help you realise how much you have learned since you started learning the language.

3. Create goals. I talk more about this in the next section of this chapter.

4. Take away the most boring parts of learning. I talk about this several times throughout this book as I also believe that if you do not enjoy the experience, then it will hinder your ability to learn.

5. Read more books about learning languages. There are some interesting books from polyglots around the world that give advice and/or give their stories about language learning. I have read all the following books below and I highly recommend that you try reading at least some of these books during your language learning journey.

**How to learn any language** (*Barry Farber*)
This book includes an intriguing story about Barry Farber's language learning life. This book is now a few decades old; therefore, the small amount of advice about learning language is out of date as he talks about using tape recorders. With the advent of MP3 players, downloadable files and the internet, the language learning environment is now completely different. I still highly recommend this book as the story he gives in this book gave me lots of motivation to continue to learn my languages. The last chapter of this book also gives detailed information about each of the languages he has learned, which is very helpful as he describes what is

difficult and less difficult in each of these languages.

**The way of the Linguist** (*Steve Kaufmann*)
This book gives an accounted language learning journey though Steve's life while visiting and working in many different countries. Great for language learning motivation. Steve is also the founder of Lingq.com, which is one of my recommended websites, featured in this book.

**The Polyglot Project** (*Various authors*)
This book was written by many different language learners. Each person has written about their own experience of learning languages. Some of these people are studying their first language and some of them are studying their tenth. You can read about other people's experiences trying to achieve the same thing you are and gain knowledge from their mistakes that they talk about. This is an interesting read and is a great motivation boaster. Free to download or you can also purchase it from Amazon as a soft back book.

**Polyglot, How I learn languages** (*Kato Lomb*)
Kato Lomb was a successful polyglot from Hungry who could speak many languages. In this book she gives her own in-depth advice about language learning. Freely available from many websites as a download.
**Fluent in 3 months** (*Benny Lewis*)
Benny Lewis is an Irish national that started to learn his first language at 21 years old. He has now taken

on language learning as a full time career. He learns languages from intense study during 3 month as his book's title suggests. Even though I don't fully agree with his speak from day 1 policy, I still highly recommend this book as it gives lots of great advice about language learning.

**72 ways to learn Japanese/Spanish/German/French** (*Judith Meyer*)
The Author, Judith Meyer is a dedicated polyglot that can speak many languages. Her books give details about the different resources that she finds most useful to learn her languages.

6. Watch YouTube videos of other polyglots. There are now many polyglots on YouTube giving their advice about learning languages. Many of them speak several languages, sometimes even exceeding 10 languages with varying levels. Some of them regularly give language learning advice, and some of them talk in the languages they have learned or are currently learning. If they speak in the language you are learning then you should try to listen and attempt to understand these videos. Here is a list of some of the polyglots who regularly feature on YouTube that I often watch and follow:

- **Alexander Arguelles** (American) *YouTube id: profasar*
- **Richard Simcott** (British) *YouTube id: Torbyrne*
- **Luca Lampariello** (Italian) *YouTube id: poliglotta 80*

- **Felix Wang** (Belgian) *YouTube id: loki2504*
- **Steve Kaufman** (Canadian) *YouTube id: lingosteve*
- **Moses McCormick** (American) *YouTube id: laoshu505000*
- **Benny Lewis** (Irish) *YouTube id: irishpolyglot*
- **Mike Campbell** (American)*YouTube id: Glossika Training*
- **Judith Meyer** (German) *YouTube id: Sprachprofi*
- **Lindsay Dow** (British) *YouTube id: LindsayDoesLanguages*
- **Sam Gendreau** (Canadian) *YouTube id: lingholic*
- **Conor Clyne** (Ireland) *YouTube id: TheLanguageTsar*
- **Jan van der Aa** (Netherlands) *YouTube id: Jan vanderAa*
- **Anthony Lauder** (British) *YouTube id: FluentCzech*

## Setting goals

I imagine that your ultimate goal is to become fluent in the language you are learning, but I want to talk a little about using other short and long term goals as you are learning your language. This book sets its own goal for you. This goal is to get you successfully speaking in your chosen language after 12 months of study. Apart from this relatively long term goal, think about setting your own long term language goals based on why you are learning the language in the first place. Maybe the goal has already been set for you by either your job needing you to work aboard or a girlfriend or boyfriend with parents who don't speak any English. Setting short term goals is also very useful towards helping you to learn a language. These could be set every month or every few weeks. Setting short term goals helps to keep your language learning interesting as this normally involves you focusing your efforts on different aspects of language learning. For example, I sometimes set myself a goal of using one particular learning resource or method over several days or weeks. When that time period is over I will change to another method. Sometimes I will focus on learning how to have a conversation about one particular topic, by learning any new words that I need relating to that topic. If you feel you have a particular weakness in the language you are learning then set a short term goal of only learning that aspect of the language for a set period of time.

## Habits of learning

Lots of research has been made around the world about forming habits. This refers to how we can set ourselves up to create patterns of behaviour by where we will feel the need to do a task automatically. It has been shown that by carrying out a regular routine; doing the same thing everyday for a set period of time creates a lasting habit. The number of days needed to create a habit does seem to vary depending on which research centre has carried this research out. Research from 'Research UK Health Behaviour Research Centre' has shown that it can take around 66 days while research from other research centres show this number to be closer to 21 days. Even though there are disagreements between these research centres on the number of days needed for this, research does show that by doing the same task everyday for around one to two months normally does leave us with more desire to continue our new habit. Therefore if you generally suffer from motivation problems, then try to force yourself to learn everyday for the first few months and this should help you to feel more desire to continue learning after this time period.

## Making mistakes

I sometimes find that the people I have language exchanges with have little confidence in speaking English, mainly due to the fact they worry about making mistakes in the language. This is also a reason why some people never even start to speak a new language in the first place. However, in order to improve in a new language you must try to speak your new language without worrying about making mistakes. Try to forget that at school we were taught that making mistakes was a bad thing and try thinking about making mistakes in a new language as a good thing. By making mistakes in conversations you will often be corrected or if the other person didn't understand you, they will say they didn't understand. This will result in you asking questions about the vocabulary and sentence structure you had just used. Once you have found your mistakes using this method, then you will be less likely to make that same mistake again. If you succeed in not worrying about making mistakes, then your speech will be less hesitant and it will sound more natural.

## Speak without thinking too much

When you are speaking English informally, you rarely need to think about choosing the correct words to use as most of the everyday words and grammar rules that govern your language are engrained into your memory. In English, you are able to think more about the ideas of what you want to say and the words come to you naturally. Once you start to learn many of the basic words in your new language then you need to try and do the same thing here. I touched on this topic in the previous section of this chapter relating to 'not worrying about making mistakes'. Once you know many of the basic words you should try to start speaking and expressing your ideas without thinking too much about the words you are using. Instead of having long pauses in your speech, use the first words that come to your mind. You will make plenty of mistakes this way, but I have found this method is very effective for improving my speaking level quickly. It is often only when you have spoken a word out loud that you then realise you have spoken the incorrect word. If this happens, you can simply back track and say "no, I made a mistake, I want to say...". I will try to say this sentence in the language I am learning. This is one of the first sentences that I learn how to say as it is useful in these situations. If you think too much about what you are saying then you are going to start to avoid using certain words that you are not sure about using. On two occasions when you should really follow this rule is when choosing the correct gender of a word (if you are learning a language that use genders) and using tones (if you are learning a language that use tones). As discussed already, there are many languages that use genders. If we take French as an example where every noun is either feminine or masculine. This means that when you choose to use one of the French nouns, you will need to use either la (feminine) or le (masculine) with each noun. Most words that end in 'e' in French are feminine, but as the 'e' is rarely pronounced as part of the word, it is not always obvious from speaking or listening to the word. What happens if you use the wrong gender?... Nothing. The other person will still understand you perfectly in 99.99% of the cases. When I started to learn French, I tried to memorise the correct genders of every new word I was learning, but I quickly realised that this is really an impossible method for learning genders. I have since found that the best method for learning the correct genders is to not pay too much attention to the genders of words. When you come to say a noun in a conversation, just use the gender that you think is probably correct. You will start by often using the incorrect genders, but you will gradually begin to improve. The second occasion when you should try to follow this rule is with using tones in tonal languages. If we take the Thai language as an example here. Thai has 5 tones and the tone of a word determines its meaning. In this case, it is more important to use the correct tone because using the wrong tone can result in giving the wrong meaning. However, through context, your meaning will normally be understood even if some of your tones are incorrect. When you are not understood, then the other person will tell you that they have not understood. You can talk to them about what you wanted to say and you can then correct yourself.

## Fuel for the brain

As learning a language uses lots of brainpower due to the need to remember many new words and grammar rules everyday, think about changing your food diet to best help supplement your brain. Eating the right types of food has been proven to help people learn new things. Fortunately these foods are also super healthy foods that will also help with your physical and mental health. Foods that have been found to help with memory and in particular improving concentration levels are:

- **Oily fish.** This food contains omega-3 fats which are very important for brain function. Other alternatives are linseed oil, soya been oil, and walnut oil. Cod liver tablets are another alternative.

- **Pumpkin seeds.** These contain zinc that is vital for enhancing memory.

- **Wholegrain food.** Brown cereals, granary bread and brown pasta contain the right sorts of energy to help fuel your brain.

- **Blueberries.** Research has shown these are very good for your short term memory.

- **Broccoli.** This is a good source for vitamin K which is another vitamin known to improve brainpower.

- **Vitamin C.** This is thought to be good for mental health. Blackcurrants and oranges are the best sources for this vitamin.

# Language learning resources

I have tried and tested many different language learning resources with different degrees of success. Listed in this chapter are all of my preferred language learning resources that I have used in the past and cover more than one language. I have also used many other high quality resources that cover just a single language, but I have not included these resources here because it would take more space than this book could hold to cover them all. Among the resources that I have listed in this chapter, I have not tested every resource for every language;

therefore, it is possible that some of these resources for particular languages under the same brand and title will have different authors and because of this, they may not meet the same standards to the resource that I had used.

There are also some well-known language learning brands that I have tried but I have had little or no success with, because of this, I have not added them to this list.

There is a criteria of what I normally look for in a typical language learning book:

- Natural sounding and progressive dialogues. Progressive in terms of the difficulty level.
- The vocabulary used in the dialogues should be informal and they should be high frequency words.
- The dialogues should slowly introduce new words as you progress through the resource.
- The English translations for each of the new words and dialogues should be as close as possible.
- Each of the chapters should contain short, clear and concise grammar explanations. These explanations should have a connection to the dialogue featured in the same chapter.
- It's useful but not essential to have audio to go with the dialogues that sounds clear and natural.

I have placed either *(commercial)*, *(free)* or *(commercial/ free)* next to each of the resource names depending if the resource is a commercial product, a free to use resource or the resource has both free and commercial elements.

# Books

All of the below books should easily be found on the Amazon website as well as many other book selling websites.

**Teach yourself language Series** *(commercial)*
**Languages:** *60+ languages*
The Teach yourself language series comes in several different language levels. I am recommending here the 'complete series', 'perfect your language series', and 'conversation series'. These books are more comprehensive then the others Teach yourself titles. You can start using the 'complete series' books from day one as they contain basic dialogues, good quality audio, simplified grammar explanations and a good progression of difficulty from novice to intermediate.
**www.teachyourself.co.uk**

**Easy reader series** *(commercial)*
**Languages:** *French, Spanish, Italian and Arabic*
These are one of my favourite books for learning new vocabulary and new useful sentences. It uses a different style of teaching to most of the other books listed in this chapter as these books basically contain several stories without English translations. Even though the stories start with basic vocabulary, this resource is not ideal for a beginner as the stories quickly become more difficult in later chapters and there are no text translations. The audio for this book is one of the best I've used as it is very

clear and natural sounding. Unfortunately this series only comes in the four languages listed above.
www.mhprofessional.com

## Assimil *(commercial)*

**Languages:** *10+ languages*

This resource gives direct word by word translations for each of its dialogues. I find this method very useful to help me to understand how the structure of a language works. Each of the dialogues also includes very useful accompanying brief grammar explanations. The high cost of the audio is a downside to this product when comparing it to other learning resources. If you just want to purchase the book without the audio then you are still going to benefit from owning this resource.
en.assimil.com

## Colloquial Series *(commercial)*

**Languages:** *64+ languages (series 1)/ 8 languages (series 2)*

The Colloquial series is similar to the Teach yourself language series format, but this book covers more content for roughly the same cost. The content gradually becomes more difficult as you progress through each chapter. Once you have reached an intermediate level in your new language, then there is a level 2 for eight languages. A downside to these books is the overuse of formal words for some of the languages in this series.
www.routledge.com/languages/

**Living languages** *(commercial)*
**Languages:** *30+ languages*
The front cover of this book describes the content of this book to be for a complete beginner. However, I have found that this book is too difficult to start using as a beginner. The content is laid out similar to the Colloquial series and the Teach yourself series but I normally find that the content in this book is more challenging than other similar books as many of the words used in the dialogues in this resource are low frequency. I recommend using this resource when you have reached at least an upper beginner level.
www.livinglanguage.com

**Tuttle books** *(commercial)*
**Languages:** *Arabic, Hindi, Japanese, Korean, Tagalog and Vietnamese*
The Tuttle Elementary and Continuing series language learning books come in the 6 Asian languages shown above. They work in a similar way to other books shown in this section such as the Teach yourself and Colloquial books. These 6 language courses contain lots of content to help in learning your chosen language. The Tuttle company does produce language learning material for more languages under different titles but these resources are more basic and contain less content.
www.tuttlepublishing.com/language-books

**Glossika** *(commercial)*

**Languages:** *20+ languages*

This resource uses many short sentences with the translation underneath, which should be used along with the provided audio. There are no grammar explanations or vocabulary lists.

www.glossika.com

**Foreign Service Institute (FSI) Series** *(free)*

**Languages:** *45+ languages*

The FSI series is a language learning programme originally intended to help both the FBI and American military to learn foreign languages. These courses can be found freely available on many websites on the internet. The different language courses use various course structures. I have tried many of these courses and I have found some of these courses to be higher quality than others. The material for these language resources were produced in the 70s and 80s; therefore, some of the vocabulary and topics are a little old fashioned. These courses always come with audio; however, the audio is normally poor in quality, so in most cases I would only recommend this resource for reading.

www.fsi-language-courses.org

**For dummies series** *(commercial)*

**Languages:** *10+ languages*

As the title suggests, these courses are for the complete beginner. Even though I find the dialogues to be quite

short, these books do a very good job of explaining the basic concepts of a language.
www.dummies.com

**Routledge Essential Grammar** *(commercial)*
**Languages:** *40+ languages*
I have stated many times in this book that you should not place too much emphasis on learning grammar during your 12 months of study; however, I do suggest getting a grammar reference book in order to look up any grammar problems you come across. The grammar explanations in this book are explained very well and are concise. This book also contains many language sentence examples so you can use these to learn the grammar rules from context.
www.routledge.com

## Websites

**Yabla** *(commercial)*
**Languages:** *French, Spanish, Italian, German and Mandarin*
Learn languages by watching short video clips ranging from 1 to 10 minutes long. The videos also come with interactive subtitles in both English and in the foreign language you are learning. Click on the words to look up the translations in a convenient dictionary. Simple but very effective method for the lower intermediate to the advanced level language learner. You can also download the transcripts for each of the videos to print out and use to learn from.
www.yabla.com

**FluentU** *(commercial)*
**Languages:** *6 languages*
From this website you can choose from many short videos clips. Each of the videos have selectable sub-titles that can be used to find the translation of a word as well as giving you an option to view more examples of how these words are used in context.
**www.fluentu.com**

**Lingo video casts** *(commercial)*
**Languages:** *Japanese, Thai and Chinese*
Use this resource to watch short video clips from films or TV series in one of the three languages. The dialogues in the videos are then explained to you line by line by a host.
**www.thaivideocast.com**
**www.chinesevideocast.com**
**www.japanesevideocast.com**

**LingQ** *(commercial/free)*
**Languages:** *12+ languages*
This is a good website to find lots of free content to read and to listen to. The website has a paid subscription option for people wanting to use the word linking feature. You can also upload your own language learning material in order to take advantage of the features on the website as well as download learning materials already on the website.
**www.lingq.com**

**Learn with oliver** *(commercial/free)*
**Languages:** *12 languages*
This resource contains a range of foreign dictionaries. Each dictionary includes dozens of features to help with your language learning. Free to use as a dictionary and it comes with a paid subscription option that allows you to listen to the words and sentences, all of which are recorded by foreign speakers.
www.learnwitholiver.com

**Pod101** *(commercial)*
**Languages:** *30+ languages*
This website contains many dialogues that cover many different topics which are suitable for any level. I would suggest ignoring the lesson podcasts and only use the line by line dialogues and the PDF lesson notes because the podcasts use too much English. You can try this product for 7 days for free before making a decision to become a paid subscriber.
www.innovativelanguage.com

**Librivox.org** *(free)*
**Languages:** *80+ languages*
This website contains thousands of audio books that are free to download and to use. The downloads contain both the transcripts and the audio. The audio on this website has been donated by users of this website. The dialogues are often spoken quite slowly, which is helpful for listening practice for an intermediate level language learner and above.
www.librivox.org

**Tatoeba.org** *(free)*
**Languages:** *80+ languages*
This is a website designed to help language learners practice their listening skills. This website contains thousands
of audio example sentences for the user to test and practice
their listening ability. All of the sounds have been added
by other users.
**www.tatoeba.org**

**Listeningpractice.org** *(free)*
**Languages:** *15 languages*
This website uses the audio from the two previous websites,
but it uses the audio files in different ways to help people
learn languages.
**www.listeningpractice.org**

**Book 2** *(commercial/free)*
**Languages:** *30+ languages*
This website is similar to the above three websites except
the sentences are more basic as they are aimed at a beginning language learner.
**www.goethe-verlag.com/book2/**

**Open languages** *(commercial)*
**Languages:** *8 languages*
This website contains hundreds of downloadable text
dialogues that are carefully explained by hosts. This
resource has good quality content and audio.
**www.openlanguage.com/library**

# Listening/Video/Application learning aids

**Pimsleur** *(commercial)*
**Languages:** *50+ languages*
This is an audio only based language learning resource that is ideal for listening to while driving, travelling on public transport or even relaxing in the sun. These audio lessons start with basic vocabulary and then the lessons develop into sentences. This is a very effective resource as long as you use this resource along side other resources. This resource is available in more than 50 languages. Each of the courses range from 10 to 120 lessons. Each lesson lasts for 30 minutes.
**www.pimsleurdigital.com**

**Michel Thomas** *(commercial)*
**Languages:** *11 languages*
This is an audio only based learning resource. You listen to a teacher teaching two students. These two students learn new words and sentences as the teacher continuously corrects any mistakes that the students make.
**www.michelthomas.com**

**Paul Noble** *(commercial)*
**Languages:** *French, Spanish, Italian and German*
This resource is similar to the Michel Thomas method above. Listen along as the teacher talks about different topics of the language.
**www.collins.co.uk/page/**
**Learn+a+Language+with+Paul+Noble**

**Living languages** (*commercial*)

**Languages:** *30+ languages*

This resource has already been mentioned in this chapter but I have included it again here because the course also has a useful set of 'B' CDs that are purposely designed to be listened to in isolation.

**www.livinglanguage.com**

**@extra series** (*free*)

**Languages:** *French, German and Spanish*

This is a series of videos designed for the intermediate language learner. They contains almost no English speech and they do not use sub-titles, but the vocabulary used in the conversations is not overly difficult. The only place that I can find this language learning series is on YouTube. By searching on YouTube for 'extra French/German/Spanish' you will be able to find all of the episodes for this course.

**L-pack** (*free*)

**Languages:** *6 languages*

This is a video based resource that does not include any English. Follow the stories and listen along. Very good learning resource for intermediate to advanced language learners. Produced by the EU and is free to use.

**www.l-pack.eu**

**French in action/Destinos** (*commercial/free*)

**Languages:** *French and Spanish*

Both the French course (French in action) and the Spanish

course (Destinos) have been produced by the same company. They contain a series of 52 half an hour videos that tell an interesting story with the purpose of teaching you either French or Spanish. The videos become more difficult as you progress through the series. There is very little English used in the videos and there are no subtitles; therefore, these courses are only useful for someone who is at least at an intermediate language level. You can freely watch the Spanish videos on the link below but the French version is more difficult to find.

**www.learner.org/resources/series83.html** (French in action)

**www.learner.org/series/destinos/** (Destinos)

**Rosetta stone** *(commercial)*

**Languages:** *20+ languages*

As one of the more well-known language learning applications available due to the fact that the Rosetta stone resource is a heavily marketed product, I thought I should mention it here. I have tried Rosetta Stone with several languages and I have listened to the audio and followed along with the flashcard exercises. It's fun to use, which is one of it's main attractions, but using this application on its own didn't help me as much as some of the other resources featured in this chapter would have. However, I did learn lots new words and grammar structures from this resource while using it together with other resources. A downside to this product is the high cost. There are plenty of alternatives to this product so don't feel you need to purchase this language resource as part of this 12 month

language learning challenge.
**www.rosettastone.co.uk**

**Easy languages** *(free)*
**Languages:** *10+ languages*
This is a series of subtitled videos featuring presenters talking to local people from around the world, in many different languages. Great for practicing your listening ability at an intermediate to an advanced level. The speech is normally spoken at a natural speed and the hosts speak to people with varied accents, so many of the videos can be very difficult to understand for a level that is lower than intermediate.
**www.easy-languages.org**

**Slow news series** *(commercial/free)*
**Languages:** *French, Spanish, Italian, Chinese Mandarin*
Listen to news from around the world in one of the above languages. The hosts purposely speak in the languages at a slower speed in order to make it easier for the listener to understand.
**www.newsinslowitalian.com**
**www.newsinslowfrench.com**
**www.newsinslowspanish.com**
**www.slow-chinese.com**

## Resources for finding language partners
In order to learn a new language you must find as many language partners as you can. Fortunately, there are many

useful websites for doing this.

## Verbling *(commercial/free)*

This website takes advantage of the group chat on-line application, Google Hangouts. From this website you can select the available language learning chat rooms and take part in group video conversations. You will be able to meet other language learners learning the same language as you, as well as native speakers of that language. This website also gives you the option to join in with on-line group Spanish classes as well as finding language tutors.

**www.verbling.com**

## Shared talk *(free)*

This is a very good website for quickly finding native language partners. Take part in 1 to 1 conversations with people learning English by either voice or text chat. I have used this website for many years and I highly recommend it.

**www.sharedtalk.com**

## Italki *(commercial/free)*

Find on-line teachers from around the world at very good prices. This website works as the middle man by taking your money and then passing it to the language tutors. I have used this website many times for finding language tutors. This website also provides features for finding language learning partners who are other users of the website.

**www.italki.com**

**Lang-8** *(free)*

This website is primarily used for getting text corrected by natives but it is also a good place to meet new language partners.

**www.lang-8.com**


**We Speke** *(free)*

This is a relatively new website which seems to have a growing community. Choose the language that you are learning and then let the website find you suitable language partners. This website also has a feature for speaking to your chosen language partners directly on the We Speke website.

**www.wespeke.com**


**Go Speaky** *(free)*

This is a new website for finding language partners. It was still in the beta stage while writing this book but I was quickly able to find several language learning partners from it.

**www.gospeaky.com**


**HelloTalk** *(commercial/free)*

Hellotalk is a smart phone application for language learners who want to find language exchange partners. Free to download with some paid options for extra features.

**www.hellotalk.com**

### Meet up *(commercial/free)*

Meet up is a popular website for organising local meet up groups. Through this website, people from around the world have set up language groups. Use the website to check your local area for language learning meet ups in the language you are learning. You can also start your own language meet up group from this website.

**www.meetup.com**

### Conversation exchange *(free)*

This is a website containing thousands of language learner profiles from which you can either search for a language partner or you can fill out your own information on this website available for others to find you. Useful for finding language partners from around the world as well as in your local area.

**www.conversationexchange.com**

### My language exchange *(commercial/free)*

My language exchange is similar to the conversation exchange website listed previously except that this website includes a paid subscription option that gives you some added benefits.

**www.mylanguageexchange.com**

### Polyglot club *(free)*

This is another website for finding language learning partners, worldwide and locally. This website has more besides this including chat rooms, a language correction section

and question rooms for interacting with the language learning community.
**www.polyglotclub.com**

**Interpals** *(free)*
Interpals is another website for finding native language learners similar to other websites listed above.
**www.interpals.net**

**Gumtree** *(free)*
This is a useful website for finding local language tutors.
**www.gumtree.com**

**Language practice hangouts** *(free)*
You can use this google+ community to find language learning groups. This community uses volunteers who hold regular language hangouts.
**goo.gl/87tF4H**

## Advice from other websites
Listed below are some popular websites that give their own advice for learning languages.

- www.how-to-learn-any-language.com
- www.language-learning-advisor.com
- www.bbc.co.uk/languages/
- www.omniglot.com
- www.learnlangs.com
- www.freelanguage.org

- www.womenlearnthai.com
- www.about.com/education/
- www.sussex.ac.uk/languages/resources

## Language learning blogs

Below is a list of useful language learning blogs that I sometimes visit.

- www.lingholic.com
- www.thepolyglotdream.com
- www.womenlearnthai.com
- blog.thelinguist.com
- www.janvanderaa.com
- www.createyourworldbook.com/blog/
- www.omniglot.com/blog/
- www.16kinds.com
- www.mezzoguild.com
- www.everydaylanguagelearner.com
- www.lindsaydoeslanguages.com
- www.fluentin3months.com/blog-home/
- www.luvlanguages.com
- www.languagetsar.com

## Other popular language learning resources

Below is a list of useful language websites that I have tried but have not yet been mentioned. I suggest investigating each of these websites as there may be a language resource here that you will find helpful.

- www.duolingo.com
- www.ankisrs.net
- www.babbel.com
- www.langacademy.net
- www.memrise.com
- www.surfacelanguages.com
- www.learnalanguage.com
- www.languageforexchange.com

## Other useful websites

Below are some websites that I have found to be useful to my language learning in the past.

- www.audible.co.uk

  *(Find language learning audio content)*
- www.audioboom.com

  *(Good resource for free language learning audio)*
- www.opensubtitles.org

  *(Contains subtitles for thousands of films in many different languages)*
- www.translate.google.co.uk

  *(Language translation tool)*

## On-line book shops

- www.amazon.co.uk
- www.languages-direct.com
- www.barnesandnoble.com
- www.waterstones.com
- www.foyles.co.uk

- www.whsmith.co.uk

## For more information and direct links

Visit the accompanying website for this book at www. learnalanguagein1year.com/book-links.php to find direct links for each of the internet resources listed in this book as well as any updates to links that may have been made since the publication of this book. I will also include any additional resources that I have since found to be useful.

# Other language learning methods and terms

## Listening to foreign language music

I have spoken with other language learners who say they have experienced using music as a language learning method. They tell me they would listen to the same song multiple times as well as learning the downloaded lyrics until they were able to fully understand the song. I have also read several articles on language learning websites that suggest this method as a good language learning strategy. I have read the book 'Language is Music' by author and polyglot Susanna Zaraysky. In this book Susanna tries to persuade the reader that music is one of the best methods for learning languages. However, from my experience of trying to learn a language from listening to foreign language music, I have a different opinion. If you think about listening to your favourite songs in your own language, this should make you think about how difficult it is sometimes to even understand music in English. Words are often lost within the music of the song and in order to produce the rhyming lyrics, the music writer will often use unnatural sounding sentences to produce poetic lyrics that fits in with the music beat. The words used in music can sometimes be obscure, old fashioned or slang type words that are seldom used in everyday conversations. I'm also not sure about how music could be used to improve your pronunciation as a singer's pronunciation will be disguised by the action of singing and by the sound of the music. If you have a favourite foreign band that sings in the language you are learning, then listening to this might be helpful on some minimal level as long as you look up the lyrics before hand. I have tried to listen to foreign music over a long period of time in an attempt to use this method to improve my language ability, but I didn't notice any real improvements to my level. I think the time would have been better spent listening to conversational material or purpose built language learning resources.

## Watching foreign language films or TV

I once read a comment from a language learner who had just started to learn French. He said *"my goal is to only learn enough French to understand a French film"*. However, I have come to realise that a language learner needs a very high level in a language to be able to understand a foreign film without the aid of sub-titles. If you have reached a language level that enables you to easily understand a film in a foreign language, then you will have reached an advanced level. Even after I reach a level where I am able to communicate with a language partner relatively easy in their language, I will still have trouble understanding a film in that same language. I have also spoken with many people who are learning English that speak English at an advanced level, but they also say that they have trouble understanding English speaking films. I think this is due to the talking speed, the informal style of the speech and the vocabulary used with films. Using films in the early stages of learning a language isn't going to be the best use of your time unless there is a film in the language you are learning that you want to watch; in this case utilise subtitles in the language settings to maximise the language learning benefits. If your film doesn't come with subtitles for the language you are learning then you should try using the website www.open-subtitles.org. This website contains subtitles for thousands of films in many different languages. It is better to download subtitles in the language you are learning rather than use English subtitles. With English subtitles, I generally find that I read the English text more than listen to the speech. If you are able to find and download the subtitles from www.opensubtitles.org, then there are free subtitling software programmes available that you can use to match the subtitles with your film. With a quick search I found a website called www.aegisub.org that provides software for both Mac and PC (please note - I have never tried using this software). I personally own an Apple Macintosh and I use the software iSubtitle (this software is only available for the Apple Macintosh), which can be downloaded from the Apple AppStore. However, if you have the choice between speaking for 2 hours or watching a 2 hour film, then you are going to learn more in a long conversation or multiple conversations covering 2 hours, than watching a film. Watching foreign films is only going to be useful to you when you are able to understand the majority of what is being said. Otherwise the parts of the film you don't understand are just going to sound like noise to you and in turn will make it difficult for you to link the subtitles with what is actually being said. If you have purchased a film that comes with foreign subtitles, then first try to look at the subtitles and listen to the speech to check that the subtitles match with the film's speech as I have often found that the provided subtitles are different to what is being spoken. This happens even when the spoken language and subtitles are in the same language. If this is the case, then this will hinder your progress rather than help you to learn the language. The subtitles that are provided on the www.opensubtitles.org website normally provide more accurate translations than what is provided with many purchased DVDs, Blu rays and downloaded films.

## Duel readers

Duel readers refer to books that contain a story or dialogue with English text on one page and the language you are learning on the opposite page. I have purchased and tried reading several different duel reader brands in the past. I had thought these would be a useful way to connect English and foreign words together in context. However, I have found that in almost every duel reader book that I have purchased, they contain stories that were written many years ago. Sometimes 100 year old stories. This means that a lot of the vocabulary and sentence structure is going to be out of date compared with today's modern language. If you have ever read a Charles Dickens' book, then you will have noticed there are many English words used in these books that are seldom used in modern English. Another problem that I have noticed with reading duel readers is when trying to match words from one page to the other. When you reach a word in a duel reader that you don't understand, you then try to find the meaning of that word from the opposite page, but there is no indication on these pages which is the correct word, this could therefore lead to you picking the incorrect meaning. I find that by having the English translation directly underneath each of the foreign sentences as some of these books do is a more convenient method for matching the words together. In cases where there is no English translation for a foreign word, the English text will normally be restructured to use different words and this can be a little confusing for the learner. With the advent of the on-line dictionary it can be quicker to simply type a word into an on-line dictionary in order to find the correct word.

The final problem I have with using duel readers and novels in general is the fact that there will be differences in the vocabulary used in books compared with the vocabulary used in everyday speech. The goal set for this book is to be able to *speak* your chosen language to a high level. Because of this, I would not recommend using these duel readers or any formally written book. Instead of using these duel readers, use graded dialogues because they are purposely written stories for language learning. Real life conversational dialogues are also useful to read and learn from.

## Word association

Word association refers to the act of memorisation through attaching either words, sounds or characters to a visual memory, thus creating a mnemonic. This method capitalises on how our brains learn new things through visual representation. This method is particularly useful for learning a character based language such as Chinese Mandarin. You take a character that you are trying to remember and associate it with an image. An example would be with the character in Chinese Mandarin that signifies to fly (pronounced fei). This character has the vague appearance of an insect flying with wings, so I picture this in place of the character. Using word association with sounds is a more difficult challenge. It doesn't matter what image you have created for this method as I often find the stranger the image the better the memory. Don't worry if it is a very obscure odd visualisation as it is only going to be a personal thought to you. An example of using a mnemonic for a sound of a word that I have used in the past when learning Chinese Mandarin is with the word 'hu tu' meaning 'confused'. For this word, I created a picture of a confused person holding a parcel saying "who to", "who is having this parcel". Using this simple mnemonic, I easily remember this word every time I need to use it.

## Levelling up

Levelling up is a term that I had first heard on YouTube, being used by various language polyglots. This term refers to the act of taking opportunities throughout the day to use your new language with speakers of that language. People who follow this practice, actively go to particular places trying to create these sort of opportunities. Examples of this could be with shopkeepers or foreign tourists. This method would be somewhat helpful to your language progress as speaking the language is the best way to learn, but I feel lots of time is going to be wasted looking for these people when your time could be better spent speaking to people who want to be spoken with. I have never tried to actively search around my city for people to practice my languages, but I have used my languages while travelling abroad and on the occasion where my language was required in my own country. While travelling abroad, I have sometimes found myself in situations when English was not even an option as the local people did not speak

English, so I will take these opportunities by going to the local shops for the purposes of practicing that language.

## Gold list

The term gold list is a method of language learning started by a British teacher called David James. This method involves getting new words into your long term memory by writing and reviewing new words and sentences each day. As you successfully learn each of the listed words/sentences, then these words are then replaced by new words or sentences. A Google search for 'gold list language learning' will bring you many search results for this method. You may also see reviews from many people who have, by their own words, tried this method with success. If you wish to look deeper into this method, then it promises an efficient and fast way of learning. You can read more on the website www.huliganov.tv/goldlist-eu/ or view David's YouTube channel by searching for his user name 'David J. James'. I was first amazed by the claims of how fast you could learn a new language from this method. I tried using this method for several weeks, but this method didn't work well for me. I found myself getting bored very quickly and I struggled to see how this method would help me with my speech.

## Flashcards

Using cut out paper flashcards was the traditional way of learning new words before the introduction of the computer. Today, this method still remains popular, mostly used by institutes and tutors, especially among small children. Flashcards can refer to the small rectangle pieces of card with an English word on one side and the foreign translation on the other. This was a method that I often used in the past at a time when I wrongly put too much emphasis on learning lots of vocabulary and before a time when many of the language applications we see today existed such as Anki (Anki is a computer based flashcard system). Creating cut out flashcards is a time-consuming process that could be better spent using other methods. If you want to try a flashcard application, then I would suggest using Anki or one of the many other similar applications. Using a flashcard application also allows us to take advantage of spaced repetition, which is discussed further in other chapters of this book. Using flashcards as part of the learning experience is very important as long as it is used along with other methods and resources.

## Reading literature and newspapers

When you feel like you are making progress in your chosen language it can be tempting to find some well known literature in that language to read, but reading from formal books and newspapers will contain lots of formal words that at an early stage will hinder your progress rather than help. For this 12 month challenge I recommend only using graded readers, informal conversational dialogues and language resources written purposely for language learners. These types of resources contain more informal words and they should control the types of new words you are learning.

## Podcasts

Podcasts saw a limited rise in popularity around 2005 to 2008, mainly brought about by the Apple iTunes store. The popularity has decreased over recent years, but there still continues to be a steady stream of new and existing podcasts available on-line. There are many podcast directories, but the most popular directory is still the directory on the iTunes store. Below is a list of some other popular podcast directories:

- www.soundcloud.com
- www.podcastalley.com
- www.podfeed.net
- www.digitalpodcast.com

From these directories you can subscribe to new podcasts and get updated with new episodes as and when they become available. They come in many different languages and they are free to listen to. You may be able to find a podcast in the language you are learning on a topic that interests you. In this case, the hosts may speak at a speed that is too fast to fully understand at first but podcasts are most often spoken in an informal way between two or more people. They often use the sort of vocabulary that you will be learning; therefore, they are just the right sort of audio you should be listening to. These podcasts are a great resource for downloading and adding to your MP3 player to listen to while you are not sitting at your computer. If the podcast you are listening to is purposely created for language learning then it will sometimes come with downloadable transcripts that will be helpful for you to follow along with as you listen to the podcast. This will help you to pinpoint any words that you have not been able to understand by listening alone. I have found that many podcasts have been added to the website www.lingq.com. On this website the podcasts have been either transcribed by volunteers or the text has been copied from the source and then added to this website. Podcasts are only going to be useful to you if you are able to understand the majority of what is being said. Because of this, you should only listen to podcasts once you reach above an intermediate level.

## Shadowing

Shadowing is a so called language learning method that I first heard about from the polyglot Alexander Arguelles on his YouTube channel, (YouTube usename - ProfASAr) where he demonstrates how to use this method. This method involves listening to short sentences in the language you are learning and then repeating these sentences out loud while moving around. This can include simply walking back and forth or doing some other activity that involves moving around. I think this is a method that requires you to have your own space, otherwise doing this activity in front of others may look a little odd. I'm not sure about the science behind why some people think this is a good method, but it's hard to argue with what Alexander Arguelles says as he speaks more than 20 languages. I personally have never tried this method, but I suggest you have a look at Alexander Arguelle's YouTube channel or search for 'shadowing language learning' on Google if this method sounds interesting to you.

## A new word a day

I sometimes see website banners that say 'subscribe to our website today and we will send you a word of the day, everyday'. The types of words that would be sent to you are not always going to be helpful to you and will probably not relate to what you will be learning at that time; therefore, I suggest ignoring any sort of promotions such as this as they normally keep your email in order to send you lots of spam type emails to help further promote their websites.

## Talking to yourself

This method may not be for everyone as the thought of speaking out aloud to yourself when others can hear you or even if you are on your own can feel a little strange. This method often involves picking a topic and then speaking out aloud about this topic while imagining yourself with a native speaker. I have read blog posts by polyglots saying that they often do this and some language learners even pretend to interact with people on the radio and/or television. They do this by responding to what is being said while imagining the person on the radio or television is hearing what they are saying. I have tried using this method on several occasions and I have found it helped my speaking ability and confidence of speaking. I recommend trying this method as one of your short term goals by speaking to yourself in the language you are learning for a period of time over one or two weeks to see if you can feel an improvement from this method. Some scenarios you could try that I have also tried in the past are:

- Being interviewed for a job.
- Helping someone who is lost.
- Meeting someone at a bar.
- Speaking to a friend of a friend you have just met who is from a country that happens to speak the language you are learning.
- Teaching a class of people who only speak in the language you are learning.

## Recording yourself speaking

I have tried recording my voice several times while practicing reading text out aloud. I then playback the recording to myself. From these recordings, I have been able to notice some of my pronunciation mistakes. Many resources suggest doing this on a regular basis but I think recording yourself making mistakes are only going to reinforce the error that you have been making again to your memory. On top of this, using a recording device usually takes time to set up and to use each time, which is time that could be better spent learning your language. I find listening to my voice useful when I first start to learn a language for the purpose of listening to how well I am pronouncing words in a language as long as I have some audio to compare with what I am saying. However, in my opinion, a better way to achieve this would be to ask native speakers their opinions on how good your pronunciation is for quick reliable feedback.

## Learning while sleeping

If only we could learn new vocabulary by listening to language learning material while we slept. Even though research has shown that our brains continue to automatically sort and process information while we sleep, most studies show that listening to language learning material while sleeping doesn't help us learn new words. However, there has been research done from two Swiss universities who claim that under the right conditions we can learn new foreign vocabulary while sleeping as long as we only play words that we have already heard while awake and you also need to set the audio to run for the first 2 to 3 hours of sleep. I have personally never tried listening to language learning material while sleeping as I would worry more about disrupting my sleep pattern as this will make me feel tired when I'm awake and therefore my concentration levels will be lower. I have also read articles from other language learners who say they have tried listening to audio while sleeping and this method did not work them.

## Post-it notes

Many of the words that you will need to learn exist all around you in your home. Because of this, some language learners stick Post-it notes on items in their home with the word of these items written on the Post-it notes. I have personally never tried this as I believe there are only a few items in the home that are high frequency words. If this is something that sounds appealing to you then I'm sure it could help you with vocabulary for some useful words such as chair, table, cup, computer, toilet etc.

# PART TWO

# Before you start

Learning a language to an advanced level is something many people regard as an impossible achievement. It is a challenge that many people would like to accomplish but they have never had the motivation to even begin studying a language. By following the advice set out in part 2 of this book you will be starting that challenge and by using your own motivation, self belief and from the guidance of this book, you will accomplish this goal. The guidelines set out in part 2 of this book assumes you have no prior knowledge of your chosen language; therefore, even if you don't know a single word in the language that you want to learn, you can still achieve this goal in the 365 days time period. It is easy to procrastinate with learning a language as this goal requires a long time and a lot of determination to complete successfully. The time needed to achieve such a goal requires a change of daily routine, habits and in some cases a change in lifestyle because we sometimes need to free up time in our daily lives in order to accomplish such a goal. It's often difficult to know where to start with a long term goal such as learning a language. This is comparable to other long term goals such as learning an instrument, learning how to draw or writing a book. Furthermore, a challenge such as learning a language in most cases isn't going to be essential to your everyday living; therefore, you will need more motivation for this compared with most other everyday tasks. I believe this book can give you some needed motivation to help you to start and then continue learning your new language throughout the whole 12 months until you reach a point when you are going to be able to comfortably speak to a native speaker in the language you want to learn.

This chapter will make sure you are ready to start learning your new language. Following on from this chapter are then four more chapters that take you through the different language learning stages. Your learning methods will need to change at each stage of the learning process. I give you details of these changes that you will need to make in order to adapt to the ongoing increased learning level.

Before you start studying, you need be confident that the language you have chosen to learn is the language you are going to stick with until the end of the 12 months. Once this has been decided, you need to find some good quality beginner resources to have ready before you start this challenge. Rather than finding only one language learning resource you will need to find many language learning resources. Throughout these chapters, I'm going to be giving you many of my recommendations on resources you could use. The resources that I will be recommending in this book cover more than 1 language. This is because this book doesn't target 1 specific language. There will be many more quality language learning resources available to you that are only available for the 1 language you are learning; therefore, it is important to search for additional resources. While you are searching for these resources, try not to be tempted into judging resources by their covers or be tempted into buying every possible resource that you find. I have found that many language learning books that appear to be aimed at a beginner sometimes contain very little language learning content. These types of books generally include some unhelpful vocabulary lists as well as some simple language exercises. They may also include culture information for countries where the language your are learning exists, all of which is not going to be helpful towards your goal. You should search for resources containing learning material that become progressively more difficult. Each chapter will contain a vocabulary list, a short dialogue and also some brief explanations of grammar rules relating to what has been used in each of the dialogues. This sets out the standard structure of a typical resources. There are also other resources that are structured in unique ways that will also be useful. While searching for these resources, I often find it useful to look around local book shops where I will be able to flip through books available in that store. This way, I can view the product before I commit to purchasing anything. If you can't find what you are looking for in your local bookshop then the easiest method for finding language learning resources is to buy your resources on-line. Amazon and Ebay are very useful at stocking all of the books you could possible want, and many of Amazon's book listings now have a 'view inside' feature, which you can use to browse some of the introductory pages of these resources before you decide to purchase and you should of course read any reviews these products have received. You can also search on the website books.google.co.uk where, according to their figures, they have more than 30 million scanned books for you to browse. However, I mainly see older books listed on this website and buying language learning books older than 15 to 20 years can often contain old fashioned vocabulary and dialogue topics that can hinder your progress. Ideally your chosen resources will have been written in the past 10 years. When you research into buying a new resource, you should always check the publication date as some older resources update their covers in order to make them look more up to date. This had once resulted in me buying the same book twice. Additionally, you should make sure that you are buying the latest edition of a book. Language learning books sometimes release new editions that have updated vocabulary and dialogues.

Most of these language learning books will contain language learning exercises such as 'fill in the missing word', 'complete the sentences', 'rearrange the sentence to the correct order' as well as other similar exercises. However, I strongly advise that you ignore all of these types of exercises completely. I have spent many years completing language exercises, but I had noticed little or no improvement in my ability from doing this. I would also like to say that completing these types of exercises can often feel like a chore and we want to remove anything that is going to resemble the type of work that we were used to doing at school. This way, the chances of you quitting your language study will be decreased. These books also often have short and concise grammar explanations that tic- in in some way to the dialogues. These grammar rules build upon what you have read from the associated dialogues. It is a good idea to overview these rules but if any of the rules leave you confused, then it's OK to skip and forget about that grammar rule until you come across that same grammar rule again from one of your other resources; therefore, the rules will be reinforced to your memory from the many different examples and explanations. Some resources will explain these rules better than others and sometimes you will need to understand one rule before you are able to understand another rule. Because of this, when you start to learn more of the grammar rules that control the language, then the language elements start to fit together like pieces to a puzzle.

Many language learning books come with audio CDs or downloadable MP3 audio files that contain audio for the dialogues featured in the resource. This audio can be helpful towards improving your pronunciation. At the beginner stage, you will not know how the different characters and combinations of characters sound. Some resources make efforts to explain these sounds from examples taken from the English language. This is useful in most cases, but there will be times when the sound of a character or combination of characters will not exist in the English language. This is when audio is vital for helping you to reproduce the correct sounds. Sounds that do not exist in the English language will often need more practice before you are able to pronounce them correctly.

I want to now suggest to you several useful resources that you can use to begin your language study. When I start to learn a new language I will often obtain one of the language learning books from the Colloquial series range of books. Some languages in the Colloquial series have a level 1 and a level 2, but for now you only need to use the level 1 book. I recommend searching with your preferred internet book shop such as Amazon and finding out if this book is available for the language you want to learn.

You should also look at using one of the books from the Teach yourself series as a resource. These books come in a few different formats. I am recommending here the Complete [target language] or older versions of this book were called Teach yourself [target language]. The Perfect your [target language] and Teach yourself [target language] conversation are more suitable for intermediate language level learners.

My next recommendation is a book from a company called Assimil. The books that Assimil produce are one of my favourite language learning resources, so I highly recommend you use these resources if your chosen language is covered by this company. Several of the Assimil books come in a volume 1 and a volume 2, but for now you only need volume 1.

The For dummies books also produce a series of language learning books covering more than 10 languages. I have tried these books and I really liked how they are structured together and how the rules of the language are carefully explained.

One further language learning resource I would like to recommend here is a series of downloadable PDFs and audio files originally produced by the Foreign Service Institute. This resource is free to download from many websites on the internet. The website that I use to obtain this resource is www.fsi-language-courses.org. This resource covers more than 45 languages, however, the resources produced by the Foreign Service Institute for some languages are higher quality than others. I have also found that the sound quality of the accompanying audio is normally very poor; therefore, I only use the downloaded PDFs as a resource.

For a reference grammar book, I recommend using one of the Routledge Essential Grammars books. These are available at most on-line shops and they offer very useful concise grammar explanations that also include many sentence examples next to each grammar rule. I have tried many different grammar books and these have been my favourite. They provide grammar books for more than 40 languages. Other than these recommended resources, you should also search for more resources that could be useful to you. This doesn't just refer to books but also to language learning websites and language learning applications. Try searching for 'learn' followed by the language you are learning as this will give you many useful search results. You should sift through all of the spam like websites and low quality language learning websites to find some good quality internet resources. There are also more recommended resources in the 'language learning resources' chapter in this book.

As the months pass, you will need to obtain more resources that cover higher levels; therefore, as you are searching for new resources, bookmark any good quality websites that you think will be helpful to you for when your language level improves.

You also need to use an on-line dictionary. My favourite on-line dictionary is from the website www.learn-witholiver.com. If your chosen language is covered by this company, then I recommend registering your details with this website. It is free of charge to use as a dictionary and it has a paid option that will give you sound for most words and sentences in the dictionary that are produced by native speakers. If your chosen language is not covered by this company then you should still be able to find other free dictionaries as I have always been able to find multiple language dictionaries for all of the languages I have ever tried to learn or look into. You should avoid using paper dictionaries as they take more of your time to find the words your are looking for. When you start talking in your new language, you will need to quickly access new words at a moment's notice and this is when an on-line dictionary is ideal.

If you spend a long time either on public transport, driving a vehicle or doing some other daily tasks that doesn't require all of your attention, then you should have an audio resource ready to listen to. The best listening audio resource that I have used at the beginner level is a resource from a company called Pimsleur. The audio files they provide can seem to be quite expensive at first but the running time for each lesson is 30 minutes of quality audio learning material. This means that overall, per minute, this is about the same cost as other similar audio learning packages. If you don't want to buy a whole package, then the lessons can be individually purchased from www.audible. co.uk or from Apple's iTunes store. Other options for audio listening material include the Michel Thomas series, the Paul Noble series, Teach yourself conversation series, the book2 website, among others. I have listed the links for the above resources as well as more listening resource options in the 'language learning resources' chapter in this book.

If you are new to language learning then you may not have yet realised just how different most other languages are when compared to the English language in terms of both grammar and word order; therefore, you will need to be prepared to start thinking in different ways as you begin to recognise the different language patterns. To do this, you must put more focus on language immersion rather than grammar. From my experience, this more natural method of language learning is more effective, efficient and enjoyable then the traditional way of learning, which places more importance on grammar and vocabulary building. Studying grammar intensively will make you constantly think about grammar rules as you speak but we want to be able to speak a language without having to think too much about these rules.

When you know the date that you are going to start learning your new language, then make a note of this date, because a year later from this date, you are going to be speaking your new chosen language. This 12 month goal also needs to be divided into 4 quarters. Therefore, when you know your language learning start date, you then need to add a 3 month, a 6 month and a 9 month marker to a calendar in order to mark out points in time when you will need to change your learning methods based on the language stages set out in the following 4 chapters. Make notes of these dates as they will be milestones in your language learning journey.

Once you have your resources and your note pad ready and you have as much motivation as you can muster you will be ready to begin.

# Stage 1 - Months 1, 2 & 3

This chapter marks the start of your 12 month language learning challenge. From this point onwards, I will be explaining how you can start to learn a language from the very beginning; without any prior knowledge of the language you have chosen to learn.

The first step is to have a general understanding of how your new language works in terms of grammar, pronunciation and how it is written, if you have not done so already. You should also find out about any quirks or surprises that the language may throw up along the way and you can find out whether there are any similarities in the language you are learning compared to the English language. In order to do this, spend a few hours of your time reading various overviews of your chosen language. The resources that you have obtained will contain brief descriptions of the language and there are many websites offering this sort of information. Below are a few links that I have found to be helpful in the past for getting these sorts of overviews.

- www.bbc.co.uk/languages/
- www.how-to-learn-any-language.com
- www.omniglot.com
- www.freelanguage.org
- www.about.com/education/

Reading the different overviews will help you to remember and reinforce this information in your memory and having a good general overview of the language will help you to get a better idea of the challenge ahead, similar to a large blueprint or maze layout of the structure of the language that must be tackled part by part. Without this overview you may get a feeling of being a little lost as you tackle the language from one side while not knowing what lies on the other side. Knowing more about the language will also prevent you from relying on the rules that govern the English language to explain why certain parts of your new language are how they are.

Your next challenge is to get familiar with the sounds of the language and to get familiar with the language's alphabet. Many of your beginner resources will contain a pronunciation guide. Choose one of your resources that has both a pronunciation guide and also comes with audio content that gives you spoken demonstrations of all of the sounds from the language. Then spend a day or two listening to the different sounds from the language while referring to each of the individual characters and groups of characters. The difficulty level for learning the pronunciation in the language will vary depending on what language you are learning. Factors that make the pronunciation difficult include, how different the sounds are compared to your own native language and whether the sounds for the different characters change depending on the position of where the characters are placed in a word. For now, listen to each of the individual sounds for each of the characters and character combinations. Repeat each of these sounds out aloud. If you are learning a language without a romanised alphabet, then start with the language's romanised equivalent if this is an option for you. Many languages that don't use a romanised alphabet in its everyday use will still have a romanised version that can be used by people who want to learn the language. This includes languages such as Chinese Mandarin, Japanese, Thai, Russian, among others. Take one of your A4 lined sheets of paper and write down all of the language characters that have a big difference in pronunciation compared to English. Draw a line down the middle of the page. Add the foreign language on the left side of this line and add the approximate English pronunciation equivalent on the right side of this line. This sheet will now be your pronunciation cheat sheet during the next 12 months, to be used whenever you need help to remember how to pronounce any of these sounds. Continue learning the pronunciation for each of the characters until you recognise the majority of the sounds by memory. It's not important to learn every sound correctly at this stage. For the first few months your pronunciation is not going to be great and you will be pronouncing many of the sounds incorrectly. Even after several months of speaking, your pronunciation is not going to be perfect. For this point in time, you only need to pronounce the sounds well enough so that other people will be able to understand what you are saying the majority of the time. Most of the pronunciation learning will happen naturally as you learn new vocabulary, read dialogues out loud, listen to audio and speak the language. Once you believe you can pronounce the sounds in the language reasonably well, even if you are still making mistakes, then you need to move on and start to learn from your acquired resources.

The resources that you have chosen to begin studying with should state that they are for a beginning language learner. However, in my experience of using many different branded language learning materials, some self-titled beginner books are not suitable for a beginner. Therefore, if you start studying from a book that uses difficult content that leaves you feeling frustrated because it is too challenging for you as a beginner, then this will decrease your changes of success with the language and increase the chances of you quitting the language altogether before the real learning has even begun. If one of your chosen resources feels too difficult for you at any stage then you need to put that resource to the bottom of the pile and start using one of your other resources with the intent to come back to that previous resource at a later stage when you have improved your language ability. You will know a resource is too difficult for you when you are reading one of the dialogues contained in the resource and you are not able to fully grasp what the dialogue is about.

As I have already said, most of your resources will contain a typical layout containing vocabulary lists, dialogues and grammar explanations. You should use the following simple daily process when using each of your resources.

1. Start with one of your language resources from chapter 1.
2. Review the vocabulary list.
3. Read the dialogue.
4. Add any useful words from the vocabulary list and dialogue to your vocabulary list.
5. Read the Grammar explanations.
6. Go to the next chapter.
7. And so on...

If your first resource has a vocabulary list, read each word out aloud, thinking about how each word should be pronounced. Refer to your self made language pronunciation cheat sheet when needed. I have tried many different methods over the years for improving how I memorise vocabulary. The method I now use is not only the most effective way, it also requires the least amount of effort. There are a few rules that you need to follow in order to learn new words effectively. For this, you need your A4 lined notebook. Turn to one of the double page spreads and then on each of the single pages draw a line from the top centre to the bottom centre. You will be choosing words to add to these two pages that you think are going to be useful to you for when you start to practice your speaking with future language partners. Add English to the left side of each line and add the language you are learning on the right side of each of the two lines. These two pages will represent all of the new words you will be focusing on learning at that time. Important points to remember when adding new words to these lists are:

- Be very strict with the words you choose to add.
- At this stage, include only basic, high frequency words.
- Do not include any low frequency, obscure words.

Low frequency words refer to words that do not appear often in normal speech; therefore, if you don't use that word often in your own language then do not include it in your vocabulary list. Lower frequency words will be learned at the later stages. Being strict with the vocabulary you are learning is one of the most important factors for learning a new language. If you start filling your memory with words that are not going to be used again for a long time or maybe never, then you will quickly forget them and you will not leave any room on your vocabulary list for words that will be more useful to you. The reason you must only use one double page spread for this is to ensure these words are always going to be in front of you whenever you need to view and review them and they will be available, when needed. You don't want to be flicking through several pages of vocabulary lists trying to find a particular word, otherwise this word will get lost and quickly forgotten. Some of the new words that you will add to your list will be easily remembered only after a short period of time without too much effort. Conversely, you will find other words very difficult to remember and you will need to keep reviewing them multiple times from your vocabulary list until you are able to recall that word without referring to your list. Once this happens, you will be able to leave these words off your list at a time when you next update your vocabulary list.

It is important to not to include any formal words in your list at this stage as you don't need to learn them. Many languages have words that have the same general meaning, just as our English language does and often, the only differ-ence between these words is one word will be formal and the other word will be informal. You will only know if a word is formal or informal without direct feedback from a native speaker when your resource states a word is a formal or an informal version of that word. Resources will sometimes have the word 'formal' next to the formal word informing you it is a formal version of that word. If you discover that a word you have learned is formal then you should not learn this word at this early stage. You could instead learn the informal version of that word by finding it in your on-line dictionary. The online dictionaries at www.learnwitholiver.com that I recommended earlier in this book add the word 'formal' in brackets next to many formal words and I find this really helpful. The reason for not learning formal words is because it is unlikely you will need to use any kind of formal language while practicing your speaking with native speakers. This includes both speaking and listening to what your language partners are saying. Formal and informal words exist in the English language but not to the degree as some other languages. In most languages including English, you must some-times choose a particular word from a selection of words depending on:

- Who you are speaking with.
- What situation you are in.
- The context of the conversation.
- The tone of the voice.

Some languages have particular words that are used in written text but are never or are very rarely used in speech. These words can still appear in some dictionaries without any indication that these words should not used in speech, so we must bear this in mind.

Different countries that speak the same language will generally have at least several unique words that only exist in one of these countries. There are many examples of this with the English language used in the UK and in the USA, such as lift/elevator, trousers/pants, petrol/gas etc. This means that you have a choice to make when you are adding new words to your vocabulary list. Words can even change from one part of a country to another part of that same country. If you come across this problem, then you need to make a decision to either include all of the words you know exist on to your vocabulary list or stick to only learning the words from one particular country or region. Normally I choose to pick one country, this way, I don't confuse myself with multiple words for one meaning.

Your double paged vocabulary list should be open while you are studying. This way you can continuously refer to your list when needed and it is particularly important to use when you start to practice speaking. Continue to add new useful, relevant words to your list as you find them in each of the dialogues and vocabulary lists. You will continue adding words until both of the pages are full. When you have some available time, you will need to review your current vocabulary list and make a mark next to all of the words that you intend to leave off of the new list that you think you remember well enough. You also need to mark any words that you now think are not going to be useful to you in the near future. Once this has been done, cut out these two pages from your notepad and begin copying the unmarked words to your new fresh double page. I want to say again here that you need to be really strict with your decisions on what words will be kept, because you need to try and create as much space as possible for the new words that are going to be added. A small percentage of the words that you will think you have remembered and therefore leave off of your new vocabulary list will be forgotten; this is normal. If this happens, you can simply look up and find the translation for these words again and add them back onto your list. If the vocabulary list keeps filling up too quickly then you are probably adding too many low frequency words. In order to save space you can pair-up words that have opposite meanings such as *easy & difficult* and *slow & fast.* You can also match together words on the same line that have the same or very similar sounds to each other. I find this helps me to remember them both more easily. If you find that you are frequently running out of space on your vocabulary list then you should still only use the one double page spread but this time add extra text columns and fit in two vocabulary lists for each page. I normally do this once I reach the intermediate stage as the number of words I am learning per day increases. You can see examples of the lists that I have used in the past on the accompanying website at www.learnalanguagein1year. com/vocabulary-lists.php.

I have already said in a previous chapter that research shows roughly 20% of the most frequent words in most languages make up about 80% of the content from general conversational topics. It is these high frequency words we need to focus on. Learning these words will see you most quickly advance to the higher levels in the language you are learning. You can see from the below graph a visualisation of this research. It demonstrates that most of the high frequency words should be learned at the beginner and intermediate stages. It's not until the more advanced stages that we should learn the lower frequency level words.

## Word frequency graph

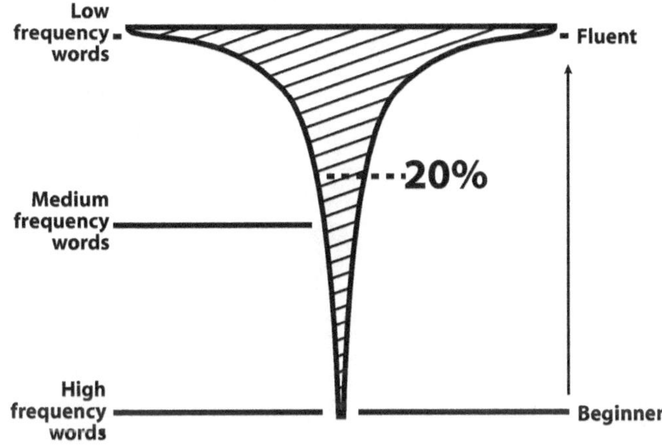


I have listed below the types of words that I would generally add to my vocabulary list as a beginner. You can use your on-line dictionary to translate these words and then add them to your own list. In each of the following chapters I will be introducing more sets of words as suggestions for you to add to your own vocabulary list.

## Stage 1 vocabulary list

| | |
|---|---|
| yes | no |
| I | and |
| but | why |
| when | what |
| this | that |
| me | often |

| | |
|---|---|
| always | sometimes |
| in addition | also |
| how are you | too |
| here | there |
| something | a little |
| a lot | hello |
| thank you | please |
| in order to | about (approximately) |
| very | about (regarding) |
| next | previous |
| you | we |
| they | to have |
| I have | you have |
| to be able to | I can |
| you can | to be |
| I am | you are |
| to go | I go |
| you go | to want |
| I want | you want |
| it is | in fact |
| unfortunately | |

Some of these words may also have multiple ways of being expressed in the language you are learning; therefore, you will need to choose the best translations from the information you have. Your vocabulary list will continuously evolve as your level in the language improves. When you start to practice speaking with your future language partners then your list will be very important to you; therefore, try to also think about this while you are selecting your new words.

When you come across English words that have multiple meanings in the language you are learning, then write a very brief explanation of that word in brackets next to the word in your vocabulary list. An example of this is with the English verb 'to know'. This word has multiple translations in many other languages depending if the verb means to know a person or to know a fact. This has been the case in all of the languages I have learned so far; therefore, I will normally write 'to know (a fact)' or 'to know (a person)' depending on which word I am learning. Another example of this is with the word 'about'. The word 'about' to mean 'approximate' and the word 'about' to mean 'concerning' is usually different words in other languages.

To help you to learn all of the words that have been added to your vocabulary list you should also add them to a computer based flashcard application that will be used routinely to review your vocabulary. I'm referring to the new modern internet and computer applications that replicate how we used the original paper flashcards. One of the more popular flashcard applications that I often use is called Anki. This can be downloaded on a PC, Mac or as an application to a smart phone or tablet from www. ankisrs.net. Once you have downloaded, installed and opened Anki, click the 'Create' button, then click on 'Add Material'. This will present you with the opportunely to add new flashcards. Add the English word to the first field, followed by the meaning of that word in the language you are learning to the second field and leave the third field blank. Finally, click the 'Add' button. Continue doing this until you have added all the words that you are currently having trouble remembering from your list. You will then be presented with some customisable options. In these options there is a field named 'new cards per day'. As a starting point, decrease this number from 20 to a lower number, around 5 to 10. This number can then be increased after your language ability starts to improve. While reviewing each flashcard, you will need to choose from a number of options depending on how easily you believe you had recognised each word. The option that you choose will determine how long it will be until you will next need to review that flashcard again. This method insures that you do not need to unnecessarily review flashcards that do not need to be reviewed. You should try to review your flashcards everyday. This daily flashcard review should not take more than 5 minutes as this flash-card application takes advantage of the spaced repetition method. Because of this, you will only review words that need to be reviewed and the flashcard application will also limit the amount of words you are shown each day. Each time you renew your A4 vocabulary list, pick out all of the words that you are having problems remembering and add them to your chosen flashcard application list. If you do not find this flashcard application particularly suited to you then there are many other flashcard websites and applications available.

Once you have picked your first resource and you have reviewed the vocabulary from that first chapter of this resource, then proceed to the first dialogue. I use a few different methods to help me absorb as much information from these dialogues as I can. Try reading the dialogues out aloud to yourself. If you don't recognise a word while you are reading these dialogues and it didn't appear in the chapter's vocabulary list, then continue reading through the rest of the dialogue without stopping mid-sentence only to forget or lose the sense of the current context of the dialogue. After you have read the dialogue, you can go back and look-up these unknown words from your on-line dictionary. If you have audio that came with a resource then you can listen to this audio after you have studied the dialogue. I find that using audio for these dialogues doesn't really help me in a big way to remember new words; there-fore, if you don't have access to audio or you don't have time to listen to the supplied audio then it is not going to be a big problem. Audio is mainly helpful at this stage for helping your pronunciation. Having the hassle of finding the correct audio piece for each of the dialogues as well as stopping and starting the audio at the correct points can take away your free study time. This time can be better spent reading and recognising patterns in the language.

Language learning resources will often contain small grammar sections that will normally relate to the chapter's dialogue. Read over these grammar explanations, but do not worry if any of these rules do not make much sense to you at this early stage. In my experience, I do not under-stand some of the more complicated grammar rules until I have learnt some other factor about the language that is linked together with this grammar rule in some way. After the grammar and dialogue sections, you will often see language exercises, but as I've stated earlier in this book, you must ignore these completely. They feel like a burden to complete and the time would be better spent continuing onto the next chapters or revising your vocabulary.

Apart from your vocabulary list in your A4 notebook, I make one more list on an A4 page. This list is used for adding any particular sentences that I come across that I think will either be useful in future conversations or sentences that are able to clearly demonstrate a particular grammar point. I have often read a sentence in a language I am learning that clearly demonstrated how a grammar rule worked better than an explanation of that grammar rule. These are the sorts of sentences that are useful to add to your list. This list can then be revised from time to time as it will help you to remember useful grammar points and practical set sentences.

In the vocabulary list featured in this chapter I added some verbs including some infinitive versions of these verbs (infinitives refers to a verb before it has been conjugated) and I also included some of the present tenses of these verbs. Most common languages conjugate their verbs and if the language you are learning uses conjugated verbs then you will need to learn these. Some languages do not use conjugated verbs; therefore, if you have chosen one of these languages then you can forget about learning conjugations all together and this would make learning verbs much easier. In the English language, there are not many changes between conjugated verbs and the English language also uses less pronouns compared to some other languages, meaning there are less conjugations in total to learn. You can see from the English verb table below (verb table example 1) that when we compare it to the Spanish verb table (verb table example 2), which uses a translated version of the same verb, then the English verb table looks relatively simple.

**Verb table example 1 - English conjugation table for 'to see'**

| Pronouns | Present | Preterite | Indicative present | Conditional | Future |
|---|---|---|---|---|---|
| I | see | saw | am seeing | would see | will see |
| he/she/it | sees | saw | is seeing | would see | will see |
| we | see | saw | are seeing | would see | will see |
| you | see | saw | are seeing | would see | will see |
| they | see | saw | are seeing | would see | will see |

Some languages use conjugated verbs that have big differences in both spelling and pronunciation and it can look daunting when you first see a typical verb table from some foreign languages. Look again at verb table example 2 which shows the Spanish conjugated verb 'ver', meaning 'to see'.

**Verb table example 2 - Spanish conjugation table for 'ver'**

| Pronouns | Present | Preterit | Imperfect | Conditional | Future |
|---|---|---|---|---|---|
| yo | veo | vi | veía | vería | veré |
| tú | ves | viste | veías | verías | verás |
| él/ella/Ud. | ve | vio | veía | vería | verá |
| nosotros | vemos | vimos | veíamos | veríamos | veremos |
| vosotros | veis | visteis | veíais | veríais | veréis |
| ellos/ellas/Uds. | ven | vieron | veían | verían | erán |

The infinitive for the above verb is 'ver'. You will see that there are many different conjugations for only this one verb and this doesn't even include the 'vos' pronoun (only used in southern countries of South America). It also doesn't include the subjective, imperative, perfect and perfect subjunctive tenses. Having to learn all of these different words is a real motivation killer and it involves a lot of memorisation. However, for the first 6 months you will only need to be learning a small section of this table. This will be the present tense and some of the past tenses for some key verbs. There is no need to learn the future tense and some of the other tenses at this early stage. On top of this, do not learn any formal pronouns for the same reason as to why we are not learning other formal words. After we have stripped out the formal pronouns and some of the tenses, the verb table will now not look as disconcerting as before. Refer to the verb table example 3 to see what this table now looks like once we have done this. If you are learning a language that has verb conjugations, then you will need to follow the similar steps in that language as I have just described here.

**Verb table example 3** - Spanish conjugation table for 'ver'

| Pronouns | Present | Preterit | Imperfect | Conditional | Future |
|---|---|---|---|---|---|
| yo | veo | vi | - | - | - |
| tú | ves | viste | - | - | - |
| él/ella. | ve | - | - | - | - |
| nosotros | vemos | - | - | - | - |
| vosotros | - | - | - | - | - |
| ellos/ellas. | ven | - | - | - | - |

Verbs for most languages can be split into two categories; regular verbs and irregular verbs. Spelling and pronunciation patterns for regular verbs can gradually be learned, so you don't need to learn every individual word. This involves learning the infinitive form of a verb and then changing a part of the infinitive depending on which pronoun and verb tense it is linked to. However, you will need to learn irregular verbs by memorisation, as there are often no relationships in spelling or pronunciation. Irregular verbs also tend to be high frequency verbs, so they are generally going to be more important to learn.

Once you have written down the useful new words to your vocabulary and flashcard lists and you have read through the dialogue and reviewed any grammar explanations. You can then continue onward through the other chapters in the same resource. Continue learning your language each day from the same resource until you reach a chapter in that resource that is too difficult for you to fully understand. When this happens, you should put this resource to the bottom of your resource pile and choose one of your other resources that you have obtained. Follow this same process of reviewing the new vocabulary, reading the dialogues and then reviewing the grammar sections. Do this until you feel you have reached a chapter in this new resource that has again become too difficult for you, and then, as before, pick one of your other resources. Continue doing this until you have followed the same process for each of your obtained language resources. Once you have finished going through all of your resources, go back to the first language learning resource that you started with and start studying with this book again from chapter 1. Review the same vocabulary, dialogues and grammar points. Lots of the information in these resources will have been remembered, but some information will have been forgotten. When you reach the section in this resource where you had to switch resources the first time, you should now find that you are able to go a little farther in that resource and be able to continue onto later chapters. Continue using this resource until the dialogues again becomes too difficult for you fully understand. If you are able to finish the resource then choose one of your other resources and start that resource again. You should continue doing this until you are able to complete all of the resources that you have. If you run out of language learning material then you should continue going over old material again as well as looking for new resources.

In the first 3 months of your language learning challenge, continue to cycle through your resources and continue reviewing your flashcards. You should also be taking opportunities to learn your language throughout the whole day. This could include listening to content on your MP3 player while you are on public transport or listening to audio while driving your car or maybe you could be listening to audio while carrying out daily chores or relaxing. Reading or listening to your resources in bed at night is also a good way to use some dead time. It is important to listen to dialogues and read content that is going to be most suitable to your level. You should be able to understand around 70 to 90% of what is being said in order to maximise the amount of information that you are learning. There are a few good resources for audio only learning which can be used from day one. These were listed in the previous chapter. Do not use the audio only learning aids that are often seen in many shops that do nothing more than repeat unrelated and impractical sentences. These audio files normally consist of a person speaking an English sentence followed by another person speaking in a rough translation of this sentence in the language you are learning followed by a short period of time with no audio for you to repeat the sentence. This kind of audio learning aid is useless for language learning as I find the sentences are rarely useful and it is very difficult to directly translate the different parts of the sentences word by word. I have experience of using these types of resources in the past and I had learned nothing from them.

This sums up the process for the first 3 months of learning your new language. As you can see, there is nothing complex about this process. It is a simple process that I have used many times based on many years of experience and it works really well for learning a language quickly and effectively.

By the end of the first 3 months you will be able to put together simple sentences relating to general conversations and you will be building on this in the following 3 months as explained in the next chapter.

## Summary

1.  Have your resources ready:
    - A4 notebook for word and sentence lists.
    - Beginner resources.
    - Grammar book.
    - Flashcard application.
    - On-line dictionary.
2.  Read an overview of the language.
3.  Work on your pronunciation from the guidance taken from your resources.
4.  Start using the resources:
    - Review the vocabulary list.
    - Read the dialogue.
    - Review vocabulary taken from the dialogue.
    - Read the grammar explanation if applicable.
    - Go to the next chapter.
5.  Start your vocabulary list in your A4 notebook based on the new words found in your resources and from the vocabulary list found in this chapter.
6.  Add words to your chosen flashcard application that you are finding difficult to remember.
7.  Review your flashcards.
8.  Add any useful sentences to a separate page in your A4 notebook.
9.  Keep going through each chapter of your resources until you find what you are reading is too difficult for you to fully understand.
10. When this happens, choose a different resource.
11. Continue this routine until you run out of resources

and then go back to the first language learning resource as well as continuing to find new resources.

12. Use your travel time to listen to audio only based language learning material.

## Key points

- Don't worry about forgetting new words.
- It's OK to make mistakes.
- Be very selective with the words you choose to add to your vocabulary list.
- If you find yourself struggling to understand a dialogue in one of your resources then move on to a different resource.
- Ignore all language exercises.
- Take advantage of any dead time to learn your language.

## Recommended resources

Recommended resources featured in this chapter.

**Books:**

- Teach yourself complete series
- Assimil volume 1
- Colloquial series 1
- For dummies series
- Foreign Service Institute (FSI) series

**Grammar:**

- Routledge Essential Grammars

**On-line dictionary:**

- www.learnwitholiver.com

**Flashcard applications:**

- www.ankisrs.net
- www.learnwitholiver.com

**Audio based learning:**

- Pimsleur
- Michel Thomas
- Paul Noble
- Book2

# Stage 2 - Months 4, 5 & 6

For this second stage, you need to make a few changes to the methods that will differ from the previous chapter. Starting from this chapter you will need to start speaking with native speakers and other language learners in your new language. You will also need to include more listening practice as well as make some other minor changes to your learning process. The amount of time that you will need to practice your speaking and listening will take away some of the time that you would have had previously used with reading from your resources.

I hope that you haven't yet given in to any urges of quitting your new language before reaching this second stage; or I hope you haven't at least yet spent any long periods of time without studying your new language. If you were able to find the time to learn your new language everyday for the past three months then that is the perfect start. If you have passed 1 or 2 days without any study then that is still going to be OK as long as this length of time was not longer than this. However, it is this second stage that will give you a greater test of how strong your will power really is because your perceived progress will start to slow down. When you reach the lower intermediate levels, the learning curve starts to flatten out. Research shows that this learning curve change happens while learning most long term tasks. I have given you suggestions on how to beat any misgivings from this slow down in previous chapters, so you shouldn't have any problems with this change of pace.

If you reach a point in time in the learning process with the feelings of quitting because you feel a particular resource is either too difficult or is giving you a feeling of being bored, then you should stop using that resource and move on to one of your other resources. If you find that you are having difficulties understanding any dialogues, then that resource is probably too difficult for you. In this case, you are not going to progress as quickly as you could do with a resource that is more suited to your level. At the same time, concentration is needed in order to take in the information. You must pay attention to what you are reading or listening to, rather than learning passively. Even though your language learning progress will feel like it has slowed down during this second stage, you should still be noticing a difference in your level around every 2 or 3 weeks. The ability to notice your improvements is very important towards your language learning because this will give you motivation to continue learning.

I will now introduce some additional resources and methods that I find very helpful at this second stage. These additional resources can be introduced along side any resources that you have not yet completed from the previous chapter. These resources are generally aimed at a higher language learning level than the recommended resources from the previous chapter. The first recommendation that I want to give you is the sequel to a resource that was already mentioned in the previous chapter. This is the Assimil volume 2 book. This book works in the same way as the Assimil volume 1 book except the vocabulary and grammar is aimed at a higher level. Unfortunately the second volume doesn't come in as many languages as the first volume so you will need to find out what languages this resource is available in. You can use the following wikipedia website to find this information - en.wikipedia.org/wiki/Assimil.

In the previous chapter, I recommended the book Teach yourself complete series resource. For this second stage, I recommend using the Teach yourself conversational series resource. This resource is simply a series of basic conversations that get progressively more difficult. There are no vocabulary lists and there are no grammar explanations featured in this resource. You will need to have your on-line dictionary available to look up any words that you do not recognise. This resource comes with some good quality audio that is useful for listening along while reading the dialogues or you can listen to the audio on its own.

Another book that I normally use as a resource at this stage is the Living language series. These are useful books to start using at this stage as they work similar to the Teach yourself complete series and the Colloquial series but the vocabulary is more difficult than other self titled beginner books.

The next recommended resource is a resource from a series of books called the Easy reader series. These books include no grammar explanations or vocabulary lists. They only include conversational dialogues that progressively becomes more difficult as you progress through the book. This book also comes with an audio CD that I highly recommend you use as the dialogues are spoken in a very natural way. Unfortunately this book only comes in 4 languages: French, Spanish, Italian and Arabic.

A final resource that I would like to recommend to you is a website called Pod101 from the website www.innovativelanguage.com. This language learning resource provides courses for more than 20 languages; therefore, your language is likely to be included. This website works similar to many of the books that you have been using as it contains dialogues, vocabulary lists and downloadable basic grammar explanations that relate to each of the associated dialogues. On top of this, each of the dialogues come with sound. This website gives you a 7 day free trial for you to test before you commit to purchasing a subscription. Each lesson also has a podcast, but I always ignore these podcasts as they use too much English.

A problem that exists with the dialogues featured in the previously mentioned resources is they are not actual real life natural conversations. Even though the writers have tried their best to make the conversations sound natural, they are conversations that have been created artificially for the purposes of learning. These dialogues have been written this way in order to include only selected high frequency words. This way, new words can be introduced in a progressive and controlled way. From my experience of first speaking in a foreign language. I found that many of the sentences, words and expressions that appeared in these types of dialogues do not often represent what are used in real life. The pronunciation and enunciation of words and sentences between what you hear from most of the audio provided by the resources compared with speech from a native speaker can also sound different. Native speakers tend not to enunciate their word fully when speaking at a normal speed, just as we do when speaking English to our friends and family. The companies who produce the language learning resources nearly always choose foreign speakers that have standard accents to create the audio, but you will experience many different types of accents from around the world that are going to sometimes sound very different from each other. Therefore, there are good and bad points with these dialogues. Because of this, it is important to also start to read and listen to natural conversations as well as continuing with the dialogues you already have. I will now introduce a few more resources that are useful for finding natural audio material to practice your listening skills. One such resource is the website www.lingq.com. Content from this website is free to listen to and to read. There is a membership option that will allow you to use the websites word linking feature. This extra feature allows you to track the amount of words that you have learned and it also keeps a record of all of the words that you are having trouble remembering. By using this feature you can then see how many words you have learned while you are studying. I have used this linking feature in the past and I had found that it was a helpful way to improve my vocabulary as well as giving me motivation to continue learning as it allowed me to keep track of my progress.

www.youtube.com is another great resource for finding natural sounding content. You can use this free popular video website to find foreign speaking videos that are going to match your ability. Try to find as many useful language videos as you can. Add each of these videos to a YouTube playlist, which is something you can do on the YouTube website once you have set up an account. You can also store the videos that you do not understand to another list for a time when you have improved your language level. You can access your YouTube account from any computer, phone or tablet that you have your YouTube account registered with. You should watch these videos multiple times until you are happy that you understand most of what is being said. I have found that people from around the world add videos to YouTube for the purposes of helping other people learn their language. There are also language learners adding videos of themselves practicing speaking a language. With this second type of video, these language learners tend to speak at a slower pace and often avoid difficult vocabulary. These are useful listening material to help you to improve your listening ability in the language. While using YouTube, search for terms such as 'speaking [target language]', or 'learning [target language]'. From these searches you should be able to find useful videos that you can use to learn from. I have also uploaded some of my own videos to www.youtube.com which you can see from my YouTube account at www.youtube.com/ user/jasonUKbristol. For every YouTube video that you find useful, you should also check to see whether that same user has other similar videos that you can also listen to. If they frequently upload videos, then you can subscribe to their channel in order to be notified of their new uploaded videos. Instead of only viewing your videos on www. youtube.com, you can also download the audio for these videos as an MP3 in order to listen to the audio in other places. The YouTube website doesn't give you an option to download their content directly, but you can achieve this from some internet browsers that have particular third-party application add-ons. The popular internet browser

Firefox has many third-party applications to choose from that does this. 'Flashgot' and 'Download helper' are two applications that I currently use. Both of these are Firefox add ons that can be found on the following website - addons.mozilla.org.

You should try to listen to your collection of audio materials many times during the next 3 months. It is particularly useful to pick several of your favourite audio/videos and repeatedly listen to them until you fully understand what is being said. If there are any words that you don't understand from the audio, then try to spell these words out in your chosen on-line language dictionary in order to find the English meaning. You can then add these words to your vocabulary list if you think they are going to be useful to you.

In the previous stage I suggested the learning resource Pimsleur. I suggested listening to level 1 of this language course. Many of the languages that this resource supports also has a level 2 and 3. If the language you are learning is also available in a level 2 in this resource then now is a good time to start listening to this level. However, as I have already stated, this language learning resource tends to be quite an expensive package and there are plenty of alternatives to this resource if this resource is out of your price range.

Another one of my favourite resources at this lower intermediate stage is a language learning website called www.yabla.com. If you are learning one of the 5 languages that this website caters for then I recommend trying this resource. It provides access to hundreds of foreign language speaking videos. It uses a simple but effective method of providing subtitles for each of the short videos in both English and in the language you are learning. You can pause the videos at any time and get translations for the vocabulary by simply clicking on the words shown in the subtitles. There are demo videos available for you to try before you make a decision to subscribe as a paid subscription is needed in order to use this website fully but the price is reasonable compared to other similar websites. This website provides a language resource for French, Spanish, Italian, German and Chinese Mandarin. However currently almost all the videos used for Chinese Mandarin are only suitable for more advanced learners, so it is not ideal for a Chinese Mandarin language learning resource at this stage.

Another language resource that works in a similar way to www.yabla.com is a website called FluentU at www.fluentu.com. This website covers resources for 6 languages. This website provides more features than www.yabla.com but this website doesn't have as many high quality videos to choose from.

An effective language learning method that I use at this level involves first finding a suitable video or audio clip that also comes with the associated downloadable transcript. From the transcript I would write down the translation from the language I am learning into English and then once I have finished doing this I will translate the text back into the language I am learning. You can use the already mentioned websites; www.yabla.com, www.Lingq. com or www.fluentu.com for this method. In order to use this method most effectively, you will need to first listen to the audio or watch the video that you have prepared. Then from the printed foreign text, try to translate this text into English on to your A4 lined paper. If you don't know the meaning of a word as you are writing the translation, then underline that word, ready to be reviewed once you have finished. After you have finished doing this, go back to review all of the words that you were not able to understand. Add any of the useful words to your vocabulary list and/or to your flashcard list. On the next day, you should go back to this video or audio content and listen to it again and then translate your previously written text from English back into the language you are learning. If you are also able to download a copy of the English transcript for this audio or video then use that instead (There is an option to download both the English and Foreign text from the www.verbling.com and www.fluentu.com websites). Continue to follow this same process throughout this second stage as well as learning from your other resources. I find that this is a particularly useful method for helping me to remember new vocabulary and it quickly improves my listening and speaking ability. I have discovered that after I have used this method for several weeks I am able to see the language I am learning in my mind's eye while I am speaking. I have read comments from other language learners who have also experienced this after using this same method. Adding new words in to your long term memory and connecting them together is the number one challenge in learning a language. By getting our brains to believe these new words are important is the best way of achieving this and I believe that by using your new language in multiple ways as shown in the methods I have just discussed, does this.

At this stage, you should also be thinking about starting to speak and communicate with others in the language you are learning. It is important to start speaking in your new language as soon as possible. Without speaking practice you are going to struggle to effectively learn your new language. Many people will find speaking with new foreign people in a language you barely know a daunting task. When you take part in your first few language exchanges it will probably feel this way, which was exactly my own experience, but I can assure you that soon after you start speaking, the nerves will stop and you will find that speaking your new language will quickly become an enjoyable and a rewarding experience. You will not yet be looking for any long term language partners. For now, it is important to be speaking with many different people in short introductory type conversations. At this stage, your vocabulary is going to be small and you will quickly run out of conversational material after only a few minutes. If you have the option of practicing your language with many different people, then you should take these opportunities. Once you have used up your language knowledge with one person and you have asked any questions that you had wanted to ask, then you should thank the person that you are speaking with for their time and move on to another person. From this method, you will find that your conversations will start to get gradually longer and longer after each and every conversation that you have. As these are language exchanges you should of course aim to help the other person with their English for a short period of time but don't allow the conversation to become an English lesson.

There are millions of people learning English in the world and I generally find that people who are learning English feel happy to be speaking with a native English speaker. You will be speaking to many people who have varying English speaking levels. When their English is very good, this is a good opportunity to ask questions in English as well as in the language you are learning. They can then correct your mistakes. If their English is poor, then they are more likely to use their own language while speaking and this is a good opportunity to practice your listening. Therefore speaking with many different types of people is better than only speaking with a select few. This is a good opportunity to improve both your listening and conversational skills. It is also a good idea to practice with English speaking language learners who are learning the same language as you are. You can exchange language learning notes with them and having a foreign language conversation with them will be easier for you because they will also be using a lower level vocabulary set and they will be talking to you at a slower speed. However, speaking with native speakers is ideal and you should be aiming to speak at every opportunity with native speakers. Don't forget to have your vocabulary list open in front of you in order to use your new words with your language partners. You have been building up your vocabulary list for conversations such as these, so your vocabulary list should continuously evolve as you improve in the language. Also keep your chosen on-line dictionary open while you are having a language exchange. This way, you can quickly look-up any words that you need to use. These are the types of words that are going to be the most useful for you to add to your vocabulary list. Be ready to write them down while you are in the middle of your language exchanges. I find that using the new words that I want to learn in a live conversation in this way, helps me to remember the words permanently or at least longer term.

In order to take part in on-line conversations you need an internet conversation tool. The most popular application for speaking on-line at the time of writing is Skype. You can download this application from the website www.skype.com and create yourself an account ID. Once you have a Skype ID you should have it ready to give to anyone who you would like to practice your language with. In the future you can either meet people on-line though many of the different websites that I will shortly be suggesting to you or you can find people in your town or city to practice your language. Although, speaking in your new language face-to-face needs more knowledge of a new language and you should wait until the forth and final stage of this 12 month challenge to try this. I will talk more about finding people in your local area in a later chapter. My favourite website for finding on-line language partners is on the website www.sharedtalk.com. This website is free to use and it is very popular with many people studying languages from around the world. Most people using this website are normally looking for English speakers to practice their English; therefore, these language learners will normally be happy to practice their language with you. This website has both a text chat option and a voice chat option but I suggest ignoring the text chat option as I have spent a long period of time using only the text chat option and I didn't see a great deal of improvement unlike the progress I experience from lots of speaking. Because of the big time differences between some countries around the world you must take into consideration what time it will be in the countries from where most people speak the language you are learning when using these conversational tools. When you believe you have found someone suitable to practice with, click their name to start a conversation. As I have already said; if there are many language partners to choose from, then at this early stage of learning, you should chat with the first language partner for a few minutes or until you run out of things to say in the language you are learning and then politely say goodbye before moving on to a different person.

Another very good website for practicing your speaking skills is on the website www.verbling.com. On this website, you can join in with groups of language learners who are all practicing languages together. However, other than groups of English, French, Spanish and occasionally Chinese, Japanese and Italian; I rarely see other language learning groups here. You can however easily start your own groups on this website and invite your own contacts from your Google+ profile as this website uses the Google hangouts application. Other than this free group chat feature, this same website also has group Spanish lessons hosted by native Spanish speaking teachers. I have tried these lessons with great success for my Spanish.

While writing this book a friend suggested to me a smart phone language learning application called HelloTalk. I now often use this application because I find it very useful for finding new language partners. This application also allows you to speak with language partners direct from your smart phone free of charge.

www.italki.com is another useful and very popular website for meeting other language learners. This website doesn't offer a solution to directly communicate with others directly on the website as per the previous websites and applications do, but from this website you can interact with language partners by sharing your Skype username. In order to find a language partner from this website, you need to first create an account, fill out your details, input the languages you are learning and then click on the personal profiles that you find in the website's data-base. From this website, it is probable that you will be able to find potential language partners in any language you want to learn as this is a very popular website. I have met many people from this website whom I now speak with as a long term language partner. I have also tried using paid tutors from this website and so far every tutor that I have used from this website has been enthusiastic, friendly and helpful. If you pay for a tutor, then 100% of the effort will be aimed at teaching you your new language instead of the language learning going both ways, which can sometimes become a language learning power struggle.

Other options for finding language partners are www.mylanguageexchange.com, www.conversationexchange.com, www.interpals.net, www.polyglotclub.com, www.gospeaky.com, www.wespeke.com and www.lang-8.com. From these websites, you can again fill out your profile for the purpose of other people finding you as well as giving you the option of being able to search for suitable profiles. Once a contact has been made you can then arrange an online chat through Skype. It's helpful to add your details to all of the websites above. Once added, you should get a steady feed of people requesting conversations with you, from which you can then pick and choose language partners based on their profiles. Aim to speak with your language partners 2 or 3 times a week during this second stage. The main focus should still be with learning new vocabulary and reading from your resources, but as you progress through the remaining two language learning stages your speaking practice will need to become more frequent.

The types of words that you are now learning from your vocabulary lists should now start to become more descriptive. Below is a new list of words that represent the types of words you should now be learning at this second stage. If there are any words on this list below that you have not yet learned then think about including them on to your vocabulary list.

**Stage 2 vocabulary list**

| | |
|---|---|
| to remember | to forget |
| strange | to worry |
| never | mostly |
| O'clock | several |
| what a pity | only joking |
| for example | concerning |
| in order to | altogether |
| interesting | to continue |
| hobby | I agree |
| of course | before |
| after | perhaps |
| to hear | the most |
| to seem | to improve |
| in the end | week |
| month | year |
| to try | useful |
| busy | free time |
| university | in fact |
| in that case | well, then |
| in addition | so |

At the end of this second stage, you will have studied your new language for 6 months in total and you should be able to: Take part in basic conversations, pronounce words in your new language better than 3 months ago and you should start to get a better understanding of how the language works in terms of how it is structured.

## Summary

1. Continue studying from the resources that you started with from the previous chapter.
2. Introduce some new resources that contain more suitable content.
3. Find audio and video that you can use to practice your listening.
4. Try translating text from the language you are learning to English and then translate it back into the language you are learning, as described in this chapter.
5. Start finding language partners.
6. Speak in your new language 2 or 3 times per week while still finding time each day to use your language resources.

## Key points

- Continue to cycle through your resources.
- The key to remembering new words is fooling your brain into thinking the words are important.
- Start looking at more natural content to listen to and to read.
- The ability to notice when you are making improvements is important for your motivation and also for tailoring your learning methods.
- Listen to audio and video clips multiple times until you clearly understand what is being said.

# Recommended resources
Recommended resources featured in this chapter.

**Books:**
- Easy reader series
- Teach yourself conversational
- Assimil Volume 2
- Living langauges

**Websites:**
- www.lingq.com
- www.innovativelanguage.com
- www.goethe-verlag.com/book2/
- www.yabla.com
- www.fluentu.com
- www.openlanguage.com/library
- www.youtube.com

**Websites/applications for speaking practice:**
- www.sharedtalk.com
- www.verbling.com
- www.italki.com
- www.mylanguageexchange.com
- www.conversationexchange.com
- www.interpals.net
- www.hellotalk.com
- www.polyglotclub.com
- www.gospeaky.com
- www.wespeke.com

- www.lang-8.com

# Stage 3 -
# Months 7, 8 & 9

You've reached the half way point of your challenge. From this third stage onwards you will still need to:

- Continue to cycle through all of your resources.
- Take part in language exchanges.
- Revise your vocabulary.
- Practice listening to natural sounding content.

You should now have completed many of your resources and they will now feel easier to read and understand than they did 3 months ago. You should be able to understand most of the dialogues from your resources without needing to refer to your vocabulary lists as often as before. From this mid-way point you will now need to take your language level up another notch. In order to do this, you will again need to step outside of your language learning comfort zone for speaking, reading and listening. You will again need to find additional resources that are going to be aimed at a higher level than before.

My first recommendation for a new resource at this third stage is the Colloquial series level 2 resource. This book is similar to the Colloquial series level 1 resource, except the vocabulary frequency level is lower and this book uses dialogues that uses grammar aimed at a higher level. The next resource that I want to recommend is another Teach yourself resource. This version of the Teach yourself resource is called Teach yourself - Perfect your language. This resource is similar to the other Teach yourself resources except the content is aimed at a higher level.

All of your new resources from this stage should be aimed at language learners with at least an intermediate level ability. Therefore, when you search for new language learning material, you should search for resources aimed at the intermediate language learner. If you are still using your resources obtained from the previous 3 months then you should stay with these, unless you feel they are too easy for you, in which case it is important to find higher level learning material. Your new intermediate level resources will offer many new conversational topics and increased vocabulary difficulty. However, I have found that many intermediate language learning books try to introduce formal and low frequency words, but you should still try to avoid these kinds of words. As I have mentioned in earlier chapters of this book; if you are unsure about whether a word is going to be useful to you, then you should think about how often you use that word in your own language. You could also try asking native speakers whether a word you want to learn is used in daily speech as I have often learned a new word to later find that when I try to use that word in a conversation with a native speaker, I am told that this word is either not used in everyday speech or there is a more suitable, less formal version of this word that I should be using instead. In these cases, I will discard the first word and replace it with the new word. Speaking the language to native speakers is the best source for gaining this sort of information as it is a great way of receiving direct and instant feedback.

You should sometimes try to refer back to your older resources that you were using in the first 3 months of this challenge and read them in a more natural way. This will help you to realise how far you have come in only a short space of time and it will also help you to recognise many of the basic grammar structures. This is because once I am familiar with much of the vocabulary in a dialogue then my attention is more focused on the building blocks of what makes the sentence fit together and from this, I am able to recognise the grammar rules and patterns featured in these dialogues more clearly than before.

Along side studying any new introduced resources you also need to start focusing more of your time listening to natural speech and more of your time speaking in your new language. Listening and speaking practice should now start to gradually replace the time you use for studying with your resources. You could think about cutting down the amount of time you spend on reading dialogues to 3 to 4 days per week while you increase the amount of time you spend on speaking practice and listening to language learning audio.

For new listening material, you should continue to find more audio and video clips to match your language level from www.youtube.com, www.lingq.com, www.yabla.com and www.fluentu.com as well as using any of the other recommended resources that I have already mentioned that contain audio or video. There are two new video/audio based language resources I would like to mention at this stage that are suitable for someone at an intermediate level. One resource that I have used for both French and Spanish is a language learning comedy series called @extra. This is a series of 13 half an hour episodes that follow a story of a man who is from the USA going to France, Spain or Germany to learn, French, Spanish or German depending on which language you are learning. From these videos you see the trouble he gets himself into while struggling with the language.

The next language learning video series that I want to recommend to you is available to use and download for free from the website www.l-pack.eu. This is a language learning course that comes in 7 languages and it allows you to download video, audio and the transcripts. The speech rate in these videos is close to natural speed, so it could be a little difficult for you to understand if you don't spend time studying the vocabulary and transcripts from the resource. More information about these resources is written in the 'language learning resources' chapter in this book.

You should now have experience speaking your new language with many different people. You must continue finding new people to speak the language with. From this third stage the conversations that you are taking part in should start to become longer and longer with each week that passes and you should start talking about more varied topics. This can include topics such as: details about your job, your hobbies, about how you are learning the language, about your country and the country of the other speaker. Think about the kinds of topics you would normally speak about with a new person you had met while speaking English. You could prepare new topics and questions before starting a conversation by writing down some related words onto your vocabulary list and flash-card list. You could also review your vocabulary list with your language partner by asking him or her whether you are pronouncing each of your listed words correctly. As you are reading the words from your list, try to use them in example sentences. This way you will know whether you are using these words in the correct context and there will be less confusion from your language partner with the words you are referring to. From this third stage, try to establish more regular language partners. This way, genuine conversations will start to happen.

To help keep yourself interested in the language and to also help improve certain areas of your language, start to set yourself short term language goals. You should now be familiar with all of the language basics from the language you are learning, you can start to pick and choose parts of the language that you want to focus more on. For example, you could set a 2 or 3 week time period to really concentrate on one particular resource, learning method or language skill. Once this time period is over then you could switch the emphasis onto another language related aspect. You could for example, concentrate on listening to a series of videos you found on-line by only watching and reviewing these for a week, or if the language you are learning has its own alphabet you could concentrate more on learning this for a few weeks. Setting yourself short term goals is particularly useful for improving any weaknesses you know you have in a language. By concentrating on improving certain points of your language will also improve other aspects of your language because all of the different aspects of the language are connected. This will make the language as a whole more understandable to you. While carrying out these goals it is important to continue practicing your speaking; therefore some of your time will be spent at looking for new language partners because speaking the language is still going to be the most important language learning factor that will improve your language level as quickly as possible.

As per the previous chapters, I have listed the kinds of words which I think you should be adding to your vocabulary list at this stage.

## Stage 3 vocabulary list

| | |
|---|---|
| to plan | to seem |
| to decide | next time |
| polite | last time |
| to prefer | to change |
| confidence | to choose |
| confused | at first |
| conversation | to take notes |
| funny | to correct |
| recently | hard working |
| to visit | topic |
| convenient | to explain |
| sentence | to mix |
| no matter | reason |
| to add | week |
| in order to | to practice |
| normally | strange |
| to try | recently |
| to improve | except |
| progress | in addition |
| a plan | |

By the end of this third stage, the rate by which you are learning should now start to be quickening and you should start to notice more improvements from week to week.

## Summary

1. Continue to cycle through your language learning resources.
2. Introduce higher level language learning resources.
3. Set short term language goals.
4. Start to decrease the amount of time you are learning from resources and replace this with more listening and speaking practice.
5. Start having longer language exchanges about more varied topics.

## Key points

- Keep moving out of your language learning comfort zone with your resources.
- Start setting language goals.
- It is very important to speak as often as you can.
- Start speaking about more varied topics.

## Resources

Recommended resources featured in this chapter.

### Books:

- Colloquial series 2
- Teach yourself - Perfect your language

### Video based learning:

- @extra series
- www.l-pack.eu

# Stage 4 - Months 10, 11 & 12

This is the final stage of your language learning challenge. During this final stage, you will be concentrating on improving your speaking and listening ability. From this forth stage you should now be able to communicate with native speakers and other language learners on a number of basic, everyday topics. It is important to continue finding more language partners who are willing to speak the language you are learning back to you. This would be the most natural way to improve your listening ability. A few methods that you could adopt to help to improve both your speaking and listening ability is by speaking together with your language partner for a period of time in one language and then for both of you to speak the same amount of time in the other language or you could both speak in different languages and then swap the languages after a set period of time. This is a good method for improving your listening ability as well as helping the other person with their English; therefore, both language learners will leave the conversation happy. Another way to practice your speaking and listening ability would be to use an on-line tutor. This will only be beneficial to you if the tutor speaks the language you are learning and uses as little English as possible. I have found that www.italki.com is the best and most convenient website for finding helpful and reasonably priced tutors.

In my experience, when I first start to practice speaking in a new language, the other speaker will often only speak English as they naturally want to practice their English language with you. My language level is low at the early stages; therefore, I end up speaking a mixture of the language I want to learn as well as English, while the other person is only using English. This means, my speaking ability starts to overtake my comprehension ability. When my language level is between a beginner and an intermediate level I am still often hesitating with speaking the language and my confidence level with the language is still low. As I begin to improve my speaking level, I start to gradually speak with more and more confidence and with less hesitation. Because of this, I have noticed that gradually more and more of my language partners will speak in their own language rather than use English, which seems to correspond with my ability to speak well in a new language. Maybe this is because they believe that you will understand them better if they speak in their own language rather than struggle along with their English. When this first starts to happen, I often struggle to understand what the other person is saying. However, after a couple of months of doing this, I start to feel an improvement in my comprehension ability as I am able to practice my listening more often. I also find that, sometimes it only takes a very well pronounced opening sentence in a language exchange for the other person to begin using their own language. However, the experience with each person you meet will be different. The English level of language partners can also depend on which language you are learning as I have had different experiences with the various languages that I have tried learning. Generally speaking, my experience with learning French was that most people who I practiced speaking with already spoke good English, particularly northern African countries, although there were still many exceptions to this. With the Chinese Mandarin language there seemed to be a big mixture of different levels, from almost no knowledge of English to speaking English to a near fluent level. With the Spanish language, the English language level was generally lower. With the Thai language, most people that I spoke with had a low level of English.

In order to continue improving your speaking ability, you should try to continue introducing new topics. If you start talking about a new topic, then you will often find that your language partner will also join in the same conversation. There will be times when you will have lots of awkward pauses in a language exchange, even if you are normally naturally confident in speaking with people in your own language. With the extra complication of only using a limited amount of vocabulary and needing to think more about what you are saying, can sometimes make this an issue. If you find yourself not knowing what to say, then you could have a list of topics to refer to for backup. If you often go back to the same topics, then this is fine because you are still communicating in your new language; therefore you will still be learning. I always feel that I have made an improvement in a new language after every single language exchange that I have. This is where the common expression 'practice makes perfect' is very true. You can refer to the 'Language learning secrets' chapter in this book to find my suggestions of some conversational topics that I often use.

Participating in group conversations is also another way to start discussing a greater variety of topics. Other people will join in with these groups and then start their own topics. As discussed earlier in this book, you can join group chats with www.verbling.com, Skype and Google hangouts. You can use Skype as a way to take part in group chats by selecting several contacts from your Skype contact list and then click on the plus button for each of the contacts that you want to add. You can also view organised Skype group language exchanges on the website community.skype.com where you can search for 'learn languages' followed by the language you are learning. You can also use Google hangouts for group chats by starting a Google+ account, then from the search menu inside the community section of your Google+ account search for 'language groups [target language]'. From this search you may find scheduled language discussion groups for the language you are learning. There are many language learning groups available on the internet that hold regular language hangouts. From these language groups you can participate and chat with others on a regular bases. You can also find Google language group hangouts listed on the Google+ community at goo.gl/87tF4H. This community uses volunteers who in their own time hold language discussion groups to help people just like you.

Even though speaking with others should be given a priority at this stage, some of your time should still be spent continuing to use your language learning resources. In order to improve your listening ability you should also continue to find audio from the already mentioned websites in order to again match your increased level.

There are additional resources that I would like to recommend in this final stage. The first recommendation is a series of 52 videos for French and Spanish language learners called French in Action (French language videos) or Destinos (Spanish language videos). Both series of videos have been produced by the same organisation. More information can be found about these two resources at www.learner.org. The next recommended resource is a series of language learning websites called news in slow French/ Spanish/Italian/Chinese. From the relevant website you can download the audio and transcripts of people talking about recent news events in that language. The hosts use almost no English, but they speak at a slower pace while trying to avoid complicated vocabulary. I've written more about this resource in the 'language learning resources' chapter in this book, where I also provide each of the website links for this resource. One more recommended video resource that I would like to mention is a collection of 3 websites for the following languages. Japanese (www. japanesevideocast.com), Chinese (www.chinesevideocast. com) and Thai (www.thaivideocast.com). These websites each contain short television/film clips. After you watch a video clip from one of these links, a host will explain to you what was said line by line. There are often many colloquial expressions introduced in these videos; there-fore, this is a useful resource for this language level.

During this final stage of the language learning experi-ence your language ability should have reached a level that will allow you to communicate in your new language on a wide number of topics with people face-to-face. Therefore, you could try to find language partners in your local area. The main difference with speaking with someone on-line compared to speaking with a language partner face-to-face is that you will really be able to experience the body language of the other person including seeing the other person's facial expressions clearly which is all part of the communication between people. Research shows that by clearly seeing the face of the other person that you are speaking with will help you to understand what is being said, as it seems we pick up visual clues from the face of the person we are speaking with while in a conversation. We should remember that body language also changes from culture to culture just as does the spoken language resulting in a new learning experience. A face-to-face language exchange could be with someone who has recently moved to your area from another country and they would like to practice their English or they could be another English speaker who is also learning the same language as you are. It will be more difficult to find a language partner in your area if you are learning one of the lesser well known languages or if you don't live in or next to a large city. A good place to start looking for other language learners in your area is on the www.gumtree.com website. You will occasionally find language exchange requests here as well as language tutors offering to teach their language to others for a small fee. I have tried using tutors from this website in the past and I have found tutors from this website are often students looking for some extra money. This means the prices are often reasonable. If you choose to use a language tutor, then you will learn more if the tutor tries to use the language you are learning as often as possible. When I have used local language tutors in the past, I have sometimes experienced tutors either using too much English or they focused too much of the lesson on learning grammar. You can learn most out of a language tutor who is going to allow you to communicate in your new language without too many interruptions and from someone who will give you feedback when needed. Language tutors should only be used when you have reached at least an upper intermediate level. This is because as a beginner, using a tutor isn't going to be any more useful to you than learning the language on your own because a language tutor is only going to be able to explain grammar rules and talk about vocabulary and short sentences with you, which is nothing more than what you can do in your own spare time. I also think that using an on-line tutor is almost as good as using a tutor face-to-face. An on-line tutor will also cost a lot less money and there also isn't going to be time and money wasted on travelling. However, using a tutor of any kind is not essential to completing this 12 month challenge as speaking with language partners would be adequate.

Another way to meet other language learners and foreign natives is with language learning groups through websites such as www.meetup.com and www.polyglotclub.com. Log into these websites and search your local area for language group meet-ups. Speaking in groups can lead to conversations on all sorts of different topics that you may not have diccussed before. These websites are very popular around the world, so you should be able to find language groups for many of the common languages in most cities in the world.

Two additional useful websites for finding local language partners are www.mylanguageexchange.com and www.conversationexchange.com. These two websites have already been mentioned in earlier chapters for finding on-line language partners, but these websites are also great for finding local language partners. These websites allow you to add your language learning requirements and personal details including the country and the city that you live in. Other language learners can then find you from your profile and you can also search for any possible language learners in your local area.

I've been talking about meeting with people face-to-face, but it is not essential to do this as video conferencing through application programmes such as Skype is the next best thing.

While you continue speaking everyday, it is important to keep your vocabulary lists up to date. You should always be asking questions about your pronunciation and about any grammar points that you are not sure about with your language partners. If you find yourself wanting to say a word while in the middle of a conversation but you do not know how to say that word then you should search for this new word using your on-line dictionary and then add it to your vocabulary list, ready for your next conversation.

Below is the final list of words for this final stage.

**Stage 4 vocabulary list**

| | |
|---|---|
| reason | to invite |
| strange | from time to time |
| celebrate | by the way |
| doesn't matter | several |
| soon | to enjoy |
| depends | aspect |

| | |
|---|---|
| context | slang |
| quality | to meet |
| various | in the world |
| to guess | dialect |
| passport | information |
| common | to research |
| to mix | to frustrate |
| experience | to intend |
| nervous | lazy |
| to notice | impossible |
| price | to imagine |
| to explain | notebook |
| download | point of view |
| secret | opposite |

## Summary

1.  Continue to cycle through your language learning resources.
2.  Look at the new recommended resources from this chapter as well as searching for additional resources for the upper intermediate level.
3.  Start to concentrate on speaking most days if not everyday.
4.  Try to find language partners and language groups in your local area.

## Key points

- Join in with more language group conversations.
- Switch conversation topics often.
- Speak the language as often as possible.

## Resources
Recommended resources featured in this chapter.


### Video based learning:
- French in action/Destinos
- www.thaivideocast.com
- www.chinesevideocast.com
- www.japanesevideocast.com


### Audio based learning:
- www.newsinslowitalian.com
- www.newsinslowfrench.com
- www.newsinslowspanish.com
- www.slow-chinese.com


### Websites for group speaking practice:
- Language practice hangouts - goo.gl/87tF4H
- www.verbling.com
- community.skype.com


### Websites for finding local language practice:
- www.gumtree.com
- www.meetup.com
- www.couchsurfing.org
- www.mylanguageexchange.com
- www.conversationexchange.com
- www.polyglotclub.com

# Language learning tips

Below is an overview of the most important factors to remember when studying a language.

- Read several overviews of the language before starting to learn that language. Look into how the language is structured and find out how similar your new language is to your mother tongue.

- Do not stick to one method of learning. Try lots of different methods that involves reading, speaking and listening.

- Do not worry about making mistakes while you are speaking with a language partner. By learning from our mistakes and we are less likely to make the same mistakes again.

- Learn as often as you can. Learning a little everyday is better than learning for 1 whole day per week. Language immersion is vital towards improving your language.

- Forget about learning most of the formal words in the language you are learning unless you need to learn formal words for a specific formal purpose.

- Speaking the language with language partners is the most important part in learning a language. Preferably with native speakers.

- Start speaking as soon as you can.

- Do not use any language learning exercises.

- Use language learning goals throughout the learning process.

- Create that habit of learning.

- Being highly selective of the vocabulary you are adding to your vocabulary list and flashcard list is one of the most important factors for learning a new language.

- Take advantage of any dead time to learn your language.

- Only read and listen to language learning material that you can understand more than 70%.

- If you find yourself struggling to understand a dialogue from one of your resources then move on to another resource with an aim to return back to this resource at a later stage.

- The ability to notice improvements in your language learning is very important as this will allow you to tailor your learning and it will give you more motivation.

- Adding words to your long term memory is the number 1 challenge in language learning. We need to get our brains to believe the words we are learning are important to us.

- When you reach the intermediate level start to listen to more real natural conversations.

- Make a list of any useful sentences you come across which clearly demonstrate useful grammar points in the language.

- Try to review your flashcards from your chosen flashcard application everyday.

# Challenge over

## Continue learning the language

If you have followed the advice from this book everyday for a year, then you should have reached a high level in the language you had wanted to learn. You should now be able to effectively communicate with native speakers on many different topics without many problems. Your final language level will depend on many factors including the difficulty of the language and the amount of time you were able to put into your challenge, but whatever your chosen language was, your level should be good enough to add your new language onto your CV as at least a conversational speaker. If you have come this far with your new language, then it is my hope that you will continue to take your new language to yet another level. If you choose to continue improving your new language ability, then the good news is the process will now become easier because you are now able to speak to natives conversationally and this will help you to improve your level. If you choose to stop learning for a long period of time before reaching a fluent level then unfortunately in my experience, my language level does suffer from a long period of time without using the language; but your level can quickly be brought back to a high level by a short period of intense language study over several days. Because of this, if you have not used your new language for a long period of time and you expect to be going travelling to a country that speaks your new language then it would be a good idea to spend a week or two revising the language. However, I have found that once reaching a more advanced level in a language, then even after a long period of time with no practice, I will still be able to retain most of the language to memory and I will generally not have many problems with communication.

I believe the methods shown in this book will increase your learning rate, however some methods that work really well for me may not work in the same way for you; therefore try to pay attention each week to how much you have learned from all of the different resources or methods that you will be using and adjust your learning methods to best suit you.

## Do you want to learn an additional language?

Once I had the satisfaction of being able to speak confidently in my first foreign language, I felt the urge to try learning yet more languages. I quickly realised that learning another new language felt easier than the previous language. I now know that this applies predominantly to related languages, but this even seemed to happen when the languages were not related. There are several possible reasons for this. One reason could be because of your improved learning process. You will have been learning a language through trial and error; therefore, for the next language, you will know more about the learning methods that didn't work quite so well for you. Another possible reason has to do with exercising parts of your brain that help retain vocabulary, which is a theory believed by many people. I also tend to agree with this theory as I've experienced improved memory in my daily life after I started to be able to speak well in my second language.

If you continue to choose yet more languages, then each new language will become increasingly easier and more enjoyable. This has been my experience.

# Interesting language facts

- The number of languages estimated in the world is 6,800. 2200 of these languages exist in Asia, and around 800 of these from India alone.

- 2400 languages in the world are classed as being endangered with one dying every 14 days.

- The oldest written language is believed to have been written about 45000BC.

- Language isolates are languages that at present have not been shown to be related to any other language. These include Basque, Korean, Ainu and Burushaski.

- Esperanto is the most widely spoken artificial language in the world with around 1,000,000 speakers worldwide.

- There have been around 200 known artificial languages created for the purpose of communication between humans.

- The 6 official languages of the UN are English, Russian, French, Spanish, Mandarin and Arabic.

- The US has no official language.

- The UK has 8 living spoken indigenous languages. One of these languages is Cornish. Although, there are thought to be less than 500 speakers of this language.

- The official language on the Isle of Man is Manx.

- After the Norman conquest of 1066, French became the dominant language in England for 300 years.

- The welsh language is spoken by over 5,000 people in a region in Argentina.

- 80% of African languages have no written form.

- The oldest written language still to be in existence today is thought to be either Chinese or Greek. Dating back to around 1500BC.

- The longest word in the English language is pneumonoultramicroscopicsilicovolcanoconiosis, meaning lung disease caused by inhaling very fine ash and sand dust.

- More than 50% of the world speak more than 1 language.

- In Europe; UK and Ireland have the lowest rates of bilingualism.

- Somalia is the only African country in which the entire population speaks the same language, Somali.

- Russian is written in the Cyrillic script which is based on the Greek alphabet.

- The word 'alphabet' comes from the first two letters of the Greek alphabet - alpha and beta.

# About the author

My Name is Jason Eyermann. I was Born on April 1980 in the city of Bristol which is situated in the southwest of England. I also grew up in Bristol and I currently live in Bristol.

At the time of writing this book I was working as a self-employed graphic designer under the company name Aspire create. You can find my company website at www. aspirecreate.co.uk. Even though I normally have a busy work schedule, I set aside some time on most days for my hobbies, one being language learning.

I have been learning languages as a hobby for more

than 15 years. Over this period of time I have been able to improve my language learning by trying many different methods and resources while paying attention to any noticeable improvements in order to make my language learning more efficient and enjoyable.

# The end

Thank you very much for purchasing this book. I had spent most week-ends and many week-day evenings researching, writing and editing this book for more than a year an a half. If you find any errors in this book or if you have any comments you would like to send me relating to this book then please send your email to jason@learnalanguagein1year.com. I can then update any errors in the eBook version of this book as well as make any updates to possible further editions to the printed book. If you would like to send me a review of this book that I can place on the accompanying website then that would be very helpful.

Otherwise, if you have purchased this book from the Amazon website or from one of the other on-line book stores, then by adding a review to one of these websites would also be much appreciated.

You can contact me or follow me on the following language learning and social media websites:

- **Email:** jason@learnalanguagein1year.co.uk
- **YouTube:** www.youtube.com/user/jasonUKbristol
- **Twitter:** www.twitter.com/aspire_create
- **Google+:** plus.google.com/+JasonEyermann
- **italki:** www.italki.com/jasoneyermann